PRAISE FOR *INSPIRE ACCOUNTABLITY*

"I hear this from executives about millennials all the time: 'Why won't they just do their job?' If you really want to know why, and what you can do to unleash the power of a segment of the workforce that will dominate the next decade, read this book. Ken did a great job explaining the problem and how a new way of thinking is necessary to solve it. I particularly like the practical tips instructing executives on which kinds of questions to be asking employees and using the parent/child dialogue to explain a different mind-set for diagnosing issues. This was an exciting read for me because I employ 170 people in my two companies, most of whom are millennials. Reading Ken's book gave me some new insight on how to inspire accountability in my teams here and abroad. I worked with Ken as my coach for many years. Ken helped me to become a more effective CEO and the results have been outstanding. I recommend Ken to any CEO and executive that is serious about finding a thought partner that can help them take their company to the next level."

—Scott Smigler

Founder and CEO, Exclusive Concepts, Inc.

Cofounder and Managing Director, Grow by Data

"Ken Estridge is a rare combination of seasoned executive coach and entrepreneur. He has personal experience building and running startups, as well as decades of experience in coaching executives, business owners, and entrepreneurs. He is a true expert on executive development and high-performance collaboration. He advised me in my business ventures for over seven years. Whether you are a C-suite executive at a Fortune 100 company, a venture capitalist with your own fund, or the leader of a tech venture, Estridge's insights into how to get the best from your teams *in his book,* Inspire Accountability, *will give you valuable insights for your business.*

—Nova Spivack

Founder and CEO, Magical

"*Ken Estridge's book,* Inspire Accountability, *provides meaningful and useful insights and advice based on Ken's years of experience as a business leader and executive coach across a wide range of industries. Ken has a deep understanding of human nature and behavior, team dynamics, and how organizations function. Through real-life anecdotes, he provides context making his message enjoyable to read, easy to comprehend, relatable, and relevant. Most importantly, the management tools and examples he provides are very useful for formulating and implementing the business strategies his coaching advises. The benefits of Ken's coaching are tangible and readily realized. Ken offers both the wisdom of a seasoned professional and the fresh perspectives of an engaged, empathetic, and inquisitive mind. His material is current to today's evolving business environment, addressing issues such as technology and changing social norms.*

I worked with Ken as my executive coach for two years and feel the time I spent with him was very worthwhile. Those who learn from Ken have the added benefit of being able to teach from Ken. I highly recommend to any executive that he or she learn from this book and live by its lessons."

—David Shrestinian

Senior Vice President of Project Development, Skanska USA

"Inspire Accountability *is a compelling, refreshing, and practical approach to getting the results you want through people. If you manage others then this book is a must read. And if you manage people who manage others, buy copies for everyone. This book literally can help you and your organization achieve results you never imagined."*

—Elizabeth B. Crook

CEO, Orchard Advisors

Author, Live Large: The Achiever's Guide to What's Next

"Employees must know the answers to two fundamental, yet rarely answered, questions that drive accountability: 'What exactly am I expected to accomplish or produce?' and 'How will I be measured against that?' Both are routinely absent, overcomplicated, and/or under com-municated. Managers wonder why performance is subpar, and employees wonder why their bosses don't give them more clarity. Inspire Account-ability *prescribes the solution: a straightforward, practical process to improve communication, accountability, and engagement. If you manage people and want them to feel engaged and accomplish more, read this book."*

—Mark E. Green

Author, Activators—A CEO's Guide to Clearer Thinking and Getting Things Done

Advisor, Speaker, and CEO Coach

"If you want to improve accountability with your teams, you must read this book. Ken makes a great case for how we need to think entirely differ-ently about the role of the leader in creating accountability in today's age of millennial workers. He puts the burden of accountability right where it belongs, on the leader. With his 7Cs model, Ken provides a practical guide for the questions a leader needs to ask to understand how to get the high accountability they desire to achieve their goals."

—Kevin Lawrence

Author, Your Oxygen Mask First: 17 Habits to Help High Achievers Survive & Thrive in Leadership & Life

Advisor to CEOs and Executive Teams

"Inspire Accountability *is an important book that decodes the patterns inherent in being accountable and inspiring others to be accountable. Accountability is perhaps the most vital leadership attribute. Ken Estridge's 7Cs of Accountability is a brilliant tool to troubleshoot the accountability dynamic we all face—I will be implementing them in my firm immediately to further improve our culture and results. Move this book to the top of your reading list!"*

—Rick Crossland

Author, The A Player

"Inspire Accountability *hits the nail on the head in describing the challenges that CEOs and business owners are currently confronting with hiring and retaining the best talent. It also effectively deals with the constant conversations going on in many companies about 'how to hire and manage these millennials.'*

With over twenty-five years of consulting and coaching both big and small companies, I have seen the two big challenges of accountability and communication in all organizations—including the military and especially in government and nonprofits. I have also witnessed the success of those companies that had inspirational leaders, like Bill Hewlett and Dave Packard at HP, with totally engaged and inspired employees. This was contrasted with Admiral Rickover's Nuclear Submarine Navy, which hired the best, but had huge turnover problems due to the culture of strong accountability but little empowerment or inspiration.

Today, the problem is that most leadership is not well trained or experienced with what Ken defines as the manager's mission to enable, empower, and inspire. Those skills are not taught in school or at home, and seldom at small companies. The concepts that are trained at the big companies are often based on historical paradigms and military training which, while effective at accountability, is often uninspiring.

So, what are leaders to do? I believe the answer is to read Ken's book, take his assessment of the 7Cs, and move forward with training and implementing these key ideas on how to enable, empower, and inspire employees. It is the formula for a transformation into a new and better culture that can be effective in today's challenging hiring and training environment for getting and retaining the best talent."

—Tom Meyer

President, Ventom Holdings, LLC

"Few business books have inspired me to seriously reflect on how I ran my business and what I could have done better as much as Inspire Accountability. *If only Ken had written it sooner! The 7Cs is a simple, but well-defined roadmap for achieving a more satisfying workplace for both managers and employees, while also increasing profitability. Regardless of the size of your business, this book will make a positive difference in all the metrics that matter!"*

—Jill Greenberg

Former Managing Partner, Financial Strategy, Inc.

Executive in Residence, Brandeis University

"I have worked with and followed Ken Estridge for almost two decades. As a former CEO, he lives with a philosophy of accountability. I've watched him helped hundreds of senior leaders get the most from their teams and deliver superior results and achieve tremendous accountability and consistency in his own life. Ken is someone you want to read about. He is also someone you can trust. Top C-suite executives seek him out for his help and insight. I'm so pleased he took the time to write down so many of the ideas that have helped shape so many successful companies and

their inspirational leaders. I loved his summary of the 7Cs and think the compensation box is the one most often disconnected!"

—Barb Singer

CEO, Executive Core

"Ken has created a masterful work with Inspire Accountability. *He brings a framework based on research, experience, and application to business leaders, all in an easy and enjoyable read. Having known Ken for nearly a decade as an executive business coach, I can personally vouch for the wisdom, pragmatism, and credible foundation of the 7Cs method he has created, and the tools he is contributing to our global business community."*

—Keith Cupp

Founder and CEO, Gravitas Impact Premium Coaches

"As a CEO of an early-stage company, nearly all of my employees are millennials. They are amazing, bright, and motivated, but Ken is spot-on in his assessment of their attitude towards accountability. The 7Cs method in Ken's book, Inspire Accountability, *gives you a workable plan to connect with employees who always seem to be out of step with the company's goals and culture."*

—Susan MacKay, PhD

CEO, Cerahelix, Inc.

"Ken Estridge's new book, Inspire Accountability, *is a treasure trove of insights and practical techniques for addressing what he brilliantly identifies as the key necessary ingredient for effective leadership, motivation, and productivity: obtaining accountability. He also points out that while obtaining accountability from staff has always been an essential task for*

managers, it is particularly challenging now in the age of millennials. Ken brings both the problems faced by managers and effective solutions to life with stories and examples drawn from his extensive experience as a master executive coach. Bottom line: I highly recommend this valuable book to any manager or leader hoping to inspire their organization and people to fulfill their potential and achieve greater levels of success."

—Tana Pesso

Master Executive Coach

Author, First Invite Love In: 40 Time-Tested Tools For Creating A More Compassionate Life

"Having experienced Ken's keen intellect and insight firsthand, I am not surprised that he has delivered an insightful and interesting look at one of the biggest business disruptors facing corporate America today. Inspire Accountability *tackles the thorny question of how to inspire accountability and loyalty in this epic time of the changing of the guard between baby boomers and millennials and the balance of power and culture shift it brings between employee and employer. The 7Cs approach, along with straightforward examples and explanations, provides an erudite game plan for you as a leader and, by extension, your enterprise to survive and thrive in this new age of millennials."*

—Ken Shuler

DVP of a large retail company

"Leadership is all about getting things done through people. In today's technology age of millennial workers, leaders need a whole new way of thinking and behaving. Ken's book, Inspire Accountability, *changes the leadership paradigm of demanding accountability and holding people accountable through fear (or else management), to inspiring accountabil-*

ity through appreciative dialog. He explains how the creation of a culture that makes it safe for people to really tell you what they think, especially if it means challenging the dictates of authority, is required to get high employee engagement and accountability from educated workers. Ken puts the burden of accountability right where it belongs—on the leader—and provides a practical guide for the questions a leader needs to ask to understand how to get the high accountability they desire to achieve their goals. I've had the pleasure of working with Ken as my executive coach for a year. In this time, I have gained an understanding of the strategies he describes in this book to improve my leadership skills. In all cases, his techniques and recommendations have proved successful in my leadership and career development."

—Christopher Durand

Director of Cloud Security Integration Services, Verizon

"I found Inspire Accountability *to be both intriguing and useful. It is full of good, common-sense advice for creating accountability. Ken's advice isn't just for millennials; it works for everyone. I found myself chuckling from time to time as I realized I might just be a bit of a 'millennial' from the 70s, absent all the technology that feeds the real millennials."*

—Michael Synk

Author, Rock & Sand

Gravitas Impact Premium Coach

"I've worked with Ken as both a company and executive coach over the years which has been instrumental to the success of Forward Financing. Ken drove us to implement a best-in-class framework for accountability throughout the company. His terrific, real-world experience and ability to simplify complex ideas and initiatives made it possible for us to scale *faster than we could have imagined. Under Ken's guidance, we were able to put a recruiting and hiring process in place that has yielded some of the best talent available—while also being able to motivate and retain them. Ken's process and approach has taught me to be a better, more dynamic, leader. His book,* Inspire Accountability, *has important lessons for any leader, especially those who employ a lot of millennials as we do."*

—Justin Bakes

Cofounder and CEO, Forward Financing

"Ken has worked with our organization for a year now, and during that time he has opened our eyes on how to manage our business more effectively. We have outperformed our budgets and are looking for continuous growth in the future by using the principles Ken has instilled in us. From the staff to the executives, we couldn't be happier with how our business operates today compared to one year ago. After reading his book, Inspire Accountability, *I can safely say any business leader will come away with thoughtful ideas on how to expertly manage their organization and their team, and how to have continued success into the future."*

—Aram Hampoian

President and CEO, CoreMedical Group

"I really like the topic of Ken's book, Inspire Accountability. *It has been raised with all of my clients, so I know it's a big issue. Ken's paradigm is spot on—transitioning our mind-sets from holding others accountable to holding ourselves accountable is paramount."*

—Kenyon Blunt

Author, UnStuck

Gazelles Certified Coach

Certified Topgrading Professional

"*Ken's book,* Inspire Accountability, *will provide every leader with a great baseline and action plan to ensure they are inspiring accountability on their team and in their company. Ken has done an incredible job guiding the reader through the 7Cs of Accountability! Every leader should take the time to inspire accountability and experience the success.*"

—Shannon Byrne Susko

Serial Entrepreneur

Bestselling Author, The Metronome Effect *and* 3HAG Way

INSPIRE
ACCOUNTABILITY

KEN ESTRIDGE

INSPIRE
ACCOUNTABILITY

• • •

THE BREAKTHROUGH WORKPLACE
TRANSFORMATION FOR 21ST CENTURY
LEADERS IN THE AGE OF MILLENNIALS

Advantage®

Published by Advantage, Charleston, South Carolina.
Member of Advantage Media Group.

ADVANTAGE is a registered trademark, and the Advantage colophon is a trademark of Advantage Media Group, Inc.

Printed in the United States of America.

10 9 8 7 6 5 4 3 2 1

ISBN: 978-1-64225-022-0
LCCN: 2019932648

Book design by Jamie Wise.

This publication is designed to provide accurate and authoritative information in regard to the subject matter covered. It is sold with the understanding that the publisher is not engaged in rendering legal, accounting, or other professional services. If legal advice or other expert assistance is required, the services of a competent professional person should be sought.

 Advantage Media Group is proud to be a part of the Tree Neutral® program. Tree Neutral offsets the number of trees consumed in the production and printing of this book by taking proactive steps such as planting trees in direct proportion to the number of trees used to print books. To learn more about Tree Neutral, please visit www.treeneutral.com.

Advantage Media Group is a publisher of business, self-improvement, and professional development books and online learning. We help entrepreneurs, business leaders, and professionals share their Stories, Passion, and Knowledge to help others Learn & Grow. Do you have a manuscript or book idea that you would like us to consider for publishing? Please visit advantagefamily.com or call 1.866.775.1696.

To my wife, Lee, who always leads with her heart and who has inspired me to lead with my heart. She has been asking why I haven't written a book for at least five years, so I finally broke down and wrote this book. Thanks for all your love, emotional support, encouragement, and inspiration.

TABLE OF CONTENTS

ACKNOWLEDGEMENTS

Thanks to Katherine Grayson for her support in writing this book and to the Advantage Media Group team for all of their support in editing and designing the book. Thanks to my daughter, Marion Finkle, and my marketing assistant, Karina Napier, for their inspiration and help with the design of the book cover and my new website.

Thanks to the many authors I have read over the years who have shaped my thinking. These include Patrick Lencioni, Jim Collins, Aubrey Daniels, Marshall Goldsmith, Stephen R. Covey, Simon Sinek, Robert Cialdini, Daniel Goleman, Marcus Buckingham, and many more. A special thanks to Verne Harnish, founder and CEO of the Gazelles organization and author of *Mastering the Rockefeller Habits* and *Scaling Up*, for creating wonderful leadership summits that I have attended twice a year for the past ten years. It was at these summits that I was exposed to many of the thought leaders who have shaped my thinking about leadership and management.

Thanks to Keith Cupp for your exemplary values-based servant leadership of the Gazelles International Coaching Organization for many years and the recently created Gravitas Impact Coaching Organization. You have created an environment in which coaches from around the world have generously shared their knowledge and insights. I want to especially thank my many colleagues at Gazelles International Coaches and Gravitas Impact who have shared their knowledge and experience with me over the years and helped me develop my coaching practice including Les Rubenovitch, Ron Huntington, Mark Green, Howard Shore, David Chavez, Mike Goldman, Shannon Susko, Kevin Lawrence, Elizabeth Crook, Rick Crossland, Andy Bailey, Tom Meyer, Brad Giles, Michael Synk, Bruce Eckfeldt, Bill Flynn, Cheryl Biron, Lisa Foulger, Rich Manders, Cleo

Maheux, Jerry Fons, Sean Evans, Chuck Kocher, Juan Foulks, Rick Holbrook, Jeff Dorman, Keith Upkes, Paul O'Kelly, Hazel Jackson, Ken Thiessen, Jeff Redmond, Terry Schaefer, Doug Diamond, Bob Shannon, John Cosgrove, Max Kozlovsky, and too many more to mention.

Thanks to Barbara Singer, CEO of Executive Core and former senior vice president of Lore International (acquired by KornFerry) for the many opportunities you have provided for me to coach senior executives at leading companies. Your warmth, expertise, and encouragement have been invaluable to me. Thanks to Ellen Kumata, CEO of Cambria Consulting, for the many executive coaching opportunities you have created for me over the years. Thanks also to the coaching team at KornFerry for the many coaching opportunities you have introduced me to. I have learned from all of your best practices and the use of your various assessment tools.

I also want to thank the many executives who have trusted me as their coach and shared their challenges and wisdom with me over the years. I appreciate and applaud your openness to learning and growing and I learn something new from every coaching engagement.

ABOUT THE AUTHOR

Ken Estridge is a key strategic advisor and coach to entrepreneurial CEOs and business leaders. He provides business coaching to the CEOs and senior leadership teams of dozens of mid-market and early stage growth companies. Ken is also a certified executive coach who, since 2002, has coached mid-level and C-suite executives in over twenty-five Fortune 500 companies to improve their leadership skills and increase their emotional intelligence. His prior work experience includes being a founder or cofounder of ten companies, a partner in an early stage VC firm, director of corporate finance for Ladenburg Thalman, and an investment research analyst for Fred Alger & Co. He is an active angel investor who has invested in over thirty start-ups. He received a DBA from Harvard Business School, SM from MIT Sloan and SB from MIT. He has been a guest speaker/panelist at HBS, MIT Sloan, MIT Enterprise Forum, Tufts, Babson, and Northeastern. Ken lives in Chestnut Hill, Massachusetts with his wife, Lee. He is dedicated to helping leaders maximize their success in their professional and personal lives.

INSPIRE ACCOUNTABILITY!

Success isn't just what you accomplish in your life. It's about what you inspire others to do.

—Anonymous

In my thirty-five years as a business leader, and in the years since I began to work with top-level executives to help them strengthen their own leadership skills, two things have become strikingly apparent:

One, obtaining accountability from employees—even top-level teams and reports—is not easy.

Two, even business leaders who appreciate the magic of inspiration in the enterprise may not see the connection between inspiration and *accountability.*

The fact is, as time has progressed, employees of companies large and small, domestic and global, are less likely to demonstrate full ownership of their responsibilities, and less likely to deliver hoped-for results to their bosses. Even senior-level employees, many of whom have been sent to me for coaching, disappoint their CEOs.

There are many reasons the term "nonaccountability" has been expanding in the workplace, including an employee disengagement rate that, alarmingly, has hit the 85 percent mark worldwide.[1] Yet given this new norm in working society, why is the issue of accountability particularly critical right now?

It's critical because with the advent of the millennial generation in the workplace (born 1981–1996[2]) and the ascension of millennials to positions of management and senior management, the challenge of accountability becomes one of enterprise survival.

If only we could *Inspire Accountability across our workplaces!*

TO INSPIRE ACCOUNTABILITY: A NEW URGENCY IN THE AGE OF MILLENNIALS

Millennials, more than any generation in history, defy conventional accountability standards (more about this in coming chapters), so the questions are:

- With millennials set to comprise 75 percent of the US workforce by 2025[3] (50 percent in 2020), will you survive in your position within the enterprise if you cannot obtain accountability from your millennial reports and their reports?

- Will your enterprise as a whole survive the age of millennials, or will it go the way of dinosaur companies

---

1   According to the Gallup organization's 2017 report "State of the Global Workplace," 67 percent of workers are "not engaged" while 18 percent of workers are "actively disengaged." The 85 percent total disengagement has resulted in $7 trillion in lost productivity globally.

2   According to the preponderance of sources, but the range varies depending on source.

3   Bridgette McInnis-Day, "What's the future of human resources?," World Economic Forum, April 16, 2015, https://www.weforum.org/agenda/2015/04/whats-the-future-of-human-resources/.

before it—nonadaptive businesses designed for vanished workforces?

It's no secret that millennials are now disrupting workplaces everywhere. Heavy media coverage points to turmoil especially in conventional verticals such as finance, investment banking, and law, where employers are scrambling to attract, let alone retain, the young workers. These are urgent issues. I hear such concerns daily from the senior-level executives and CEOs who have come to me for executive coaching. In response, I ask:

> IT'S NO SECRET THAT MILLENNIALS ARE NOW DISRUPTING WORKPLACES EVERYWHERE.

- "How important is it to you to change the current dynamic in your workplace and create a fully accountable leadership team—one that can ensure that its own teams are also accountable?"

- "What can you envision achieving in an enterprise where accountability permeates all ranks?"

- "Would you dare to turn old business paradigms upside down in order to thrive in the twenty-first century?"

My coaching clients universally insist that accountability is all-important. Without it, they explain, wheels spin and nothing is achieved. The vision of a twenty-first century enterprise where employees own their responsibilities and are fully accountable for their goals and tasks sends my clients' imaginations soaring. For, what could *not be achieved in such an environment?*

OUT WITH THE OLD, IN WITH THE NEW (PARADIGMS)

When I speak of paradigms that need to be flipped, which paradigms am I thinking of? Most of all, I am referring to the age-old expectation that accountability is something to be *demanded* of others; something for which one holds others responsible. If you google "accountability in the workplace," you'll see pertinent article headlines such as:

"The Right Way to Hold People Accountable"
"How to Hold Staff Accountable"
"Don't Be Afraid to Demand Accountability"
"How to Demand Accountability"
"Workplaces Demand Accountability"
"Accountability without Control: It Just Doesn't Work"
… and so on.

Still, accountability, "an obligation or willingness to accept responsibility or to account for one's actions" according to Merriam-Webster, is a state or condition of humans, not robots. And until artificial intelligence takes over the workplace (another discussion entirely), demanding accountability of humans will be about as successful an endeavor as demanding love, loyalty, passion, or sacrifice.

And yet, people willingly love and sacrifice every day. Humans also demonstrate through their actions and commitments undying loyalty and deep passion for others and for causes. People do all of these things every day of their lives, because they are *inspired* to do so.

Curiously, however, humans recoil from such actions when such behavior is *demanded* of them. They resist all measures of pressure when there simply is no clear reason or worthwhile motivation at hand.

Ah, humans! If only everything in our world—and, importantly, in our workplaces—were not reliant on the behavior of humans! If only …

- If only the behaviors of an individual were not a response to the behaviors of another individual, but existed in its own neat little vacuum and were eminently controllable.

- If only decades of command-and-control in the business place had actually worked and had not resulted in an 85 percent disengagement rate among workers.

- If only our workplaces were being manned by a generation of nineteenth century clerks like Dickens's Bob Cratchit instead of by baby boomers (1946–1964), Gen Xers (1965–1980), and now millennials (1981–1996)—the generation of young people we boomers unwittingly raised to defy our own repressive tactics in the business place.

By simply flopping the ineffectual paradigm of holding others accountable (a dead end) to one of holding *ourselves* accountable (entirely within our control), we can inspire our people to perform well for us and end the agony of putting out recurring fires when they don't. We can inspire the very accountability that has eluded us and thwarted our efforts to achieve for our companies and ourselves.

WE HAVE TO WANT TO GET INSIDE OUR EMPLOYEES' HEADS AND UNDERSTAND WHY THEY DO WHAT THEY DO.

The reality is this: *people behave in a way that, internally, is wholly logical to them.*[4] Unless we understand what is motivating

---

4   Steven Levitt and Stephen Dubner, *Freakonomics (New York: William Morrow, 2005).*

that behavior, we cannot change it. That means we have to change *our* behavior. We have to want to get inside our employees' heads and understand why they do what they do. We have to change our approach from a passive one of just making assumptions about why they behave the way they do (they're incompetent, lazy, uncaring), to a proactive one of understanding *their truth*—the personal motivations behind what they do.

Does mastering the ability to inspire accountability mean we all need sensitivity training?

ENTER THE 7CS

I'll never insist that certain managers or business leaders couldn't use some work on their emotional intelligence, what's now known as EQ. But in large part, those who manage others fail to inspire accountability not so much because of a lack of sensitivity, but because they don't know which factors directly impact accountability, and how to manage those issues.

IN BUSINESS, WE NEED OTHERS TO KEEP THEIR COMMITMENTS TO US SO THAT WE CAN KEEP THE PROMISES WE HAVE MADE TO OUR OWN SUPERIORS AND TO THE ENTERPRISE.

Certainly, there are people who are born motivators, those who have an innate understanding of human nature and a natural sense of how to inspire others to help them achieve individual, group, and company goals. News flash: they are not necessarily Mother Teresa types. Some, in fact, have purely selfish goals. Still, we don't fault them for that as long as those who assist them in those goals (their colleagues, reports, team members) benefit, too, and as long as the goals are generally well-intentioned.

Yet, most of us do not possess an inborn ability to inspire others to be accountable—that is, to own their responsibilities, commit to them, and deliver promised results that are transparent and measurable so that we can attend to our own commitments. Furthermore, we want to attend to our own commitments knowing that we needn't have eyes everywhere, every second. In business, we need others to keep their commitments to us so that we can keep the promises we have made to our own superiors and to the enterprise. We need to rely on our teams to keep things humming along while we work on the next phase of goal setting, and the next and the next. For most of us, a structured approach that helps us inspire accountability in those we rely on would be a tool of inestimable worth.

The 7Cs methodology described below is just that tool. It provides a common sense system for achieving accountability results you may never have thought possible. Employed by any manager, at any level, the 7Cs approach reverses the existing cycle detailed in the graphic below.

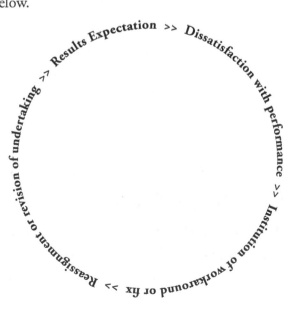

Deployed at leadership or senior management levels to impact company culture, the 7Cs method can transform a dysfunctional workplace and rewire it for greater success in the marketplace.

TAKING ACTION: TURN "AHA" MOMENTS INTO ACTIONABLE STEPS

Precisely how do you begin to change entrenched managing habits that have not been serving you and your team and organization well? You track your C revelations and turn them into a "starter" to-do list.

Set up a set of seven small notepads, text files, or recording files, each identified by its own C listed below. As you read through the following chapters, each focusing on one of the 7Cs, note specific "aha" moments to be used as launch points for your first action plan to inspire accountability. (Example: *"After managers make an assignment, they must be sure to ask: 'Do you have any questions about the work I just described?' And they must take the time to listen to and respond to questions. Let's add this to the managers' biannual review template."*)

1. Creating a **Culture** of safety for inquiry and two-way dialogue.

2. Promoting **Clarity** instead of obscuring it.

3. Caring about work **Capacity**.

4. Supporting and optimizing **Competence** in the workplace.

5. Protecting and developing job **Confidence** among employees.

6. Eliciting **Commitment** by demonstrating your own commitment to your employees and showing that you care about them.

7. Understanding the impact of **Compensation** on motivation and behavior.

WHY READ THIS BOOK NOW?

The power balance between employer and employee has shifted in the United States and across the industrialized world. Employment levels have peaked, and companies everywhere are finding it challenging to secure proficient workers, especially in major cities. Though most organizations were previously accustomed to hiring from a position of power, employees now own that edge and are less willing to make concessions. Millennials, especially, know that work opportunities abound and are not motivated by fear of unemployment as previous generations were. What's more, social media, the internet, and proliferating workplace-review websites now make it easy for potential employees to get the "inside scoop" on companies, to find out if they are good places to work. Importantly, young people today seek to retain the work/life balance that they value so highly.

COMPANIES EVERYWHERE ARE FINDING IT CHALLENGING TO SECURE PROFICIENT WORKERS

Today's job candidates are educated consumers: they

know their value in the marketplace, they know your competition, and they know what kinds of wages they can command.

In a climate like the one we have today in 2019, the burden is on you, the *employer*, to attract and retain your workforce. The 7Cs approach has been designed for just this moment in time.

WHO SHOULD READ THIS BOOK?

I routinely work with senior-level executives and leadership teams from the largest corporations in the United States, leaders of midsize firms across the country, and start-up entrepreneurs or small company CEOs who want to help their companies experience dramatic growth. These are individuals who must always keep the big picture in mind: company mission, vision, and core values. At the same time, these top-level executives are as mired in the daily struggle to navigate their responsibilities and commitments as anyone else. They must be able to delegate, move projects along, and trust that the work they hand off to others will be expedited efficiently, in a timely fashion, within budgetary parameters, and with the company's mission and values fully aligned.

These are the individuals who, in everything they do, shape their company's cultures, whether purposefully or unintentionally. For that reason alone, they are the prime focus of this book. After all, a paradigm shift emanating from the office of a senior executive has the power to inform exponential change throughout an organization. Thus, the "bang for buck" of reading this book is greatest when the reader is at or near the top of the company's org chart.

Having said that, *every* person who relies on the full accountability of those he or she manages will benefit greatly by reading *Inspire Accountability*. When those accountable to us perform at their highest levels, *we* are performing at our highest levels. Thus, mastering the 7Cs methodology that awaits within you can be the career changer that will help you serve your company and your own career path in a way you never thought possible.

Read on and get ready for a good hard look at the person who is wholly in control of getting the employee performance results you have only been dreaming about: *you*.

CHAPTER ONE

THE ACCOUNTABILITY CHALLENGE

Why can't people just do their jobs?

—in 27,300 results on a Google search

John, a recent client of mine, is a senior vice president of a Fortune 500 company.[5] When performance issues in John's area became pronounced, his boss—the executive vice president of the company—urged him to see me for executive coaching. It wasn't easy for John to make that first appointment. With not enough hours in the day to accomplish what he needed to in his own office, a coaching session would have been the last thing on his to-do list— that is, if it had been up to John, which it no longer was.

As a senior vice president, John has been directing managers below him on the org chart for longer than he'd like to admit. Things have changed quite a bit in recent years: the communications conglomerate for which he works has expanded globally and technologically, millennial employees have arrived on the scene, and some management tiers have been eliminated to save costs and flatten the organization. As his own job has expanded in all directions,

---

5   For privacy purposes, pseudonyms may be used for clients and their organizations referenced in this book.

the pressure to get results from the thousand-plus employees in his purview (many of whom are now working under him remotely) has ramped up. These days, he tells me, things are moving so fast in the company and in his uber-competitive marketplace that his stress levels have hit new highs. He doesn't have time for excuses, and he's not interested in knowing *why* people are falling short of their goals.

"I told them, 'I don't want to hear about it! Just make it happen!'" he informs me as we start to delve into his issues with his employees. I can almost feel the waves of his frustration as he leans into our conversation and implores me from across the small conference table, "Why can't people just do their jobs?"

Considering the quotation that heads up this chapter, John is not alone in his complaint. Today, accountability issues are one of the top three complaints I hear in my coaching/consulting practice. Just think about it: the 27,300 results mentioned above were fueled by people so stymied by their inability to get their employees to do their jobs that they googled cyberspace with a desperate plea for help.

WITHOUT ACCOUNTABILITY, AN EMPLOYER IS HAMMERING IN THE DARK WITH NO SENSE OF WHERE THE NAIL IS, IF A CONNECTION IS BEING MADE, IF THE NAIL IS GOING IN STRAIGHT, OR IF HE OR SHE IS CLOSE TO SMASHING HIS OR HER OWN FINGERS.

What each of these individuals is talking about is accountability in the workplace: "The obligation of an individual or organization to account for its activities, accept responsibility for them, and disclose the results in a transparent manner."[6] Without

---

6   As defined by BusinessDictionary.

accountability, an employer is hammering in the dark with no sense of where the nail is, if a connection is being made, if the nail is going in straight, or if he or she is close to smashing his or her own fingers. It's a pretty miserable feeling—experiencing that level of insecurity—when you, too, are accountable to others for the work under your direction.

And yet, though it may seem counterintuitive to you, a constantly shifting one-way conversation between manager and employee ("Just get it done!" "No, we need *this* done now!" "Where's that report I wanted last week?") serves only to ensure that your people will, sooner or later, stop being accountable to you and thus to the company.

Anyone who has ever enjoyed the classic film *Mister Roberts* can almost hear James Cagney, as the captain of the USS Reluctant, hissing, "Never mind what I told you. I'm *telling* you!" The captain countermands his own previous command in a single breath. Mutiny was certainly on the minds of the USS Reluctant crew at various points. Yet mutiny can't happen to you, can it? After all, you're not on the high seas. Besides, you're holding your people accountable for their work, right?

The real question is, how well are you succeeding? For a hint, see if any of the stories below resonate—even just a little bit.

HOW *NOT* TO INSPIRE ACCOUNTABILITY: THREE STORIES

Mark was a successful division head for a leading highway and civil construction firm in the Midwest. Over the past decade, his company grew from a small, seat-of-the-pants outfit to a company with three quarters of a billion dollars in sales, one of the largest operations in its Great Lakes regional space. Mark brought to the table his years of experience with similar heavy contractors across the industry, and that capability helped him to grow his division sales by 40 percent, to $450 million. Mark had served his company and his CEO well.

Then, with civil construction booming in the region after years of recession, top project-management talent was suddenly at a premium and tough to get in the door quickly when a project bid was clinched. What's more, the means and time to develop and promote existing project-management talent at Mark's company hadn't kept up with the CEO's push for ever-greater revenue growth. Bidding and staffing became a very real challenge for Mark.

"I feel like I'm about to topple off a high wire with no net to break my fall," he confided to me when we first met. He and his direct report were spending most of their time trying to recruit top-level people for project management, but they were doing it in an impossibly tight hiring environment. "During the recession, my CEO got used to contracting affordable talent without increasing spending on in-house hiring or training," he told me. "Now we're struggling to recruit qualified applicants, because we don't have those seasoned project management people."

I asked him, "What's your boss's reaction to that situation when you explain it to him and let him know that spending *must* bump up to get those qualified people in the door, and get others quickly trained to move up?"

Mark shook his head in dismay. "He always tells me the same thing: 'That's your job—fix it!' But then he won't free up the dollars or let me do what I need to do to get those people in the door."

Like many senior executives who survived the recession, Mark is an over-performer; he always found a way to deliver for a difficult boss used to getting top-level execution for limited support on his part. Then Mark hit a wall with a huge civil construction project that the firm won but could not adequately staff. With no talent available to contract and his own people stretched to the breaking point, his only option was to borrow manpower from another one of the company's projects already under way. While the solution was far from ideal, it at least allowed both projects to proceed, albeit not at optimal levels.

Come review time, Mark was shocked when, despite the significant level of revenue growth he continually achieved, his CEO declared he had "dropped the ball" and failed to hold his people "accountable enough." He was told to step up his game, and quickly. That's when Mark called me. I suggested that Mark, his CEO, and I work closely to improve levels of accountability across the team, but the company leader was adamant: "This is Mark's problem, not mine."

So, working together, Mark and I established that he had grown company sales dramatically and developed his own highly specialized skills in the process. He had become an outstanding leader and had been instrumental in building the organization. Now in his fifties, he was forced to admit that, after all these years, his CEO had rarely recognized what he had done well. "He only likes to tell you what you are doing wrong. He thinks it's the way to motivate you," he sighed.

With my guidance, Mark developed a clear-cut plan for moving forward to present to his boss. But time and again, his CEO was not open to a dialogue with him and cut Mark off rather than engage in a discussion about realistic solutions. Unfortunately, with each blow to his confidence, Mark had become less, not more, engaged and motivated to work hard for his company. Soon he realized that his company's mission was becoming less aligned with his own personal career mission: to make a difference for an organization that values him. Unfortunately for his boss, that realization gave him just what he needed to reassess his own career path.

Mark recently called to say that he had accepted a new job with a fast-growing and innovative outfit in the same industry. He is excited about the challenges ahead, is highly respected by his new employer, and has plenty to bring to the table. Our work together made a tremendous difference in his career path, but also in his overall sense of well-being. He benefited greatly from his coaching experience, even while we both knew who was even *more* in need of executive coaching.

TIP: Check out your watercooler. If you have never—or have not recently—viewed your own employees' comments on Glassdoor, Indeed, Comparably, WorkDesign, Vault, CareerBliss, or GreatPlaceToWork, set aside at least fifteen minutes to do so *today,* and commit to checking the sites regularly. The higher up on the org chart you are, the more likely it is that you are isolated from eye-opening employee feedback.

Mark's story reminds me of Paul, another executive I knew, who held a senior role at a Fortune 500 computer behemoth, where he was responsible for over a billion dollars in business annually. Paul was tied to his company in several ways: he was committed to the company's mission and his own personal mission to achieve recognition in his industry. And through his work for the company, he had become accustomed to providing an excellent standard of living for his family. No small detail, Paul also owned a significant quantity of options in the company.

Yet Paul was also a young man with a wife and small children who valued their time with him as he did with them. Unfortunately, his boss's attitude was "I never want to hear about your family issues. When a client says jump, you *jump*!" Paul eventually did jump—to another computer giant with a more enlightened culture that was much better aligned with the life and career he envisioned for himself.

An important part of this particular story is that Paul is not unlike the millennials now populating workforces everywhere and seeking work/life balance wherever they go. "When my daughter has a ballet recital, I want to be there," he told me. "I don't want to hear that the *only* thing that matters is the company."

Paul left money on table when he walked away from his unvested options, but his departure spoke volumes about an unfeeling and insensitive boss who had alienated one of the top people in the company. His manager could not have disengaged the company's valuable talent more effectively if he had tried. Yes, Paul was no longer accountable for his responsibilities to the enterprise, but in alienating Paul, how accountable to the organization was his *boss*?

Large enterprises are often teeming with managers who, in their misguided quest to "hold" their people accountable, are by their actions and behaviors not being accountable to the organization either, as they disengage or drive away the best employees. Destructive (including unwittingly destructive) managers exist in businesses of all sizes, and in all verticals and professions. Even the best-intentioned hires can be demotivated by such individuals.

Lydia, for instance, had been brought on board to launch a brand-new imprint for a small literary publisher on Manhattan's Lower West Side. After forty years, it became apparent to all that the company might cease to exist if it did not become competitive—especially with self-publishing seriously impacting traditional book publishing. Both the CEO and the company's second in command, Walter, agreed that a new strategy was essential. After much research, they decided to launch a self-publishing business imprint with a strong marketing arm. They conducted a thorough search for the ideal individual to lead the new division—someone with strong publishing, business publication, and marketing skills. Lydia was their top candidate, and they were delighted when she accepted their offer to head up the new effort, reporting directly to Walter.

Lydia was enthralled with her mission and excited to come to work every day—in fact, she was brimming with energy and ideas. Much to the CEO's delight, she was piloting the new initiative at record speed. The entire staff was amazed at the sheer volume of work she was able to tackle to get the new division up and running. Everyone interacted with her freely and enthusiastically, giving her the assistance she needed to reach the goal line.

Everyone, that is, except Walter, the second in command. He retreated to his office behind a closed door that could have carried the warning sign: "No Admittance … to Lydia." No matter how many times she approached Walter to discuss critical issues, either he was too busy to talk or he cut her short and dismissed her as though she were a schoolgirl. Everyone noticed that there was a problem, even the CEO, who finally decided to bring me in to interview the involved parties to see what could be done.

On site, I soon discovered that, as open and engaged in her mission as Lydia was, that's how closed Walter was to her presence. When Lydia tried to propose a different way of doing something in the new division, Walter decreed, "We don't do things that way," or, "I don't need to hear about it; that won't work." No matter how many times Lydia tried to break through to Walter to discuss issues, ask for his considered opinions on options, and offer her feedback, Walter found ways to shut her down at square one. Yet to his CEO he insisted he was 100 percent behind the new self-publishing initiative. The situation was baffling.

As it turned out, the management styles of these two individuals—Walter and Lydia—were so different that the initiative was suffering for it. Walter was "old school": He was a cerebral, introverted individual who was engrossed in his own tasks, worked "in his head," and had little time for interaction with staff. When he issued a directive, he expected it to be carried out without question or discussion. Lydia, on the other hand, was an information-seeking, inclusive manager who needed to "talk through" her decision-making process. She developed her plans of action through in-depth two-way discussions and by considering and evaluating every feasible option. In the small organization, where all staffers would be directly affected, she was not comfortable moving ahead without consensus and group approval. As she saw it, with his shut-down tactics, Walter was impeding her progress and possibly contributing to an unsuccessful launch by leaving her in the dark when she needed his input. Yet, from Walter's standpoint, Lydia's "incessant need to talk about everything" was maddening. He simply wanted her to be accountable for her own work and responsibilities, allowing him to get on with the obligations he had fulfilled for the company for forty years.

As executive coach for both Lydia and Walter, my work revealed the polarities in their working relationship, highlighting how their clashing styles hindered accountability and negatively impacted progress throughout the organization as a whole. I worked carefully and discreetly with Walter, who was somewhat resistant to the idea of coaching, but we made headway and he found the 7Cs approach to be intriguing and nonthreatening. He saw that in a changing world, his closed-door style of management would be counterproductive to everything he was hoping to achieve for the organization.

Then, because Lydia was the one most open to modifying her behavior to better mesh with Walter's management style, she and I worked through the 7Cs to help her make small, doable, yet impactful changes here and there. Our work soon allowed communication with Walter to flow and a process of inquiry to be productive. The changes Lydia made did indeed help Walter become less irascible as a manager and also helped him to feel that she was "hearing" his exhaustion with her working style. As Lydia began to relate to Walter in a manner more abbreviated and comfortable for him, he became more open to her inquiry and their two-way dialogue. And because Lydia was also a manager over numerous reports, her behavioral change made it easier for her own team members to work with her more expeditiously. The atmosphere in the workplace improved dramatically, and results (accountability) took off.

> THE PRIMARY OBLIGATION OF A MANAGER IS TO *ENABLE* HIS OR HER PEOPLE TO DELIVER THE BEST RESULTS POSSIBLE.

A MANAGER'S MISSION: ENABLING, EMPOWERING, INSPIRING

What percentage of the time do your people do what you expect them to do? Are you at a loss to understand why they are not more accountable for their work than they are at present?

The fact is, the primary obligation of a manager is to *enable* his or her people to deliver the best results possible, to achieve the overarching mission of the company. Accountability is all about delivering expected (or better) results—and better only happens when employees are wholly engaged. Managers need to count on others to do their jobs, because if employees don't deliver, the manager is culpable, too. Unfortunately, many managers do not realize that *enabling* does not mean *commanding*.

TIP: Remind yourself why you are here. It's not rocket science, but to launch your process of attitudinal change, consider creating a simple screensaver or desk placard that reminds you, "My Job Is to Help *You* Do *Your* Job." Many effective business leaders recall an early management mentor who shared this important mantra.

Life at work would be so supremely simple if enabling consisted of issuing an order and finding the task done. Throughout history, human beings have continually sought ways to get whatever they wanted accomplished. The sad story of our species is that we have employed slavery, tyranny, totalitarianism, absolute sovereignty, war, torture, bribery, and more, all to get the results we crave. Fortunately, people eventually decided that others might be induced to be more accountable if they were *paid* to do what was needed. Benefits were later offered to sweeten the pot. Rewards were added for extra motivation.

Yet here it is centuries later, and people who manage others still must expend energy to nudge their charges toward accountability. As managers, we resent that constant extra work.

You, as manager, can keep expending the energy to issue directives, hold your people accountable, express disappointment in the results, and then produce a workaround. Or you can become the manager you contracted to be, becoming accountable for your own commitment to the enterprise: to *enable* employees to deliver the best results possible, allowing both manager and workers to fulfill the overarching mission of the company.

The key here lies in the word *enable,* but you can substitute *empower, support,* or—your most effective choice—*inspire,* as you appeal to the head, heart, and gut of your workforce and become a beacon lighting a path to workplace accountability. The question is: Do you currently possess the self-awareness to guide the way? Or, like so many managers today, is your ability to inspire your staff to accountability hampered by

- years of operating within command-and-control organizational cultures,

- a negative management style inherited from others (see Chapter Two's "Trace Your Management Style Roots"), or

- an inborn or acquired deficiency in emotional intelligence (EQ) or sensitivity to others' needs?

To gauge your ability to inspire, not demand, take the following self-assessment survey and advance toward specific and positive accountability improvement.

SELF-ASSESSMENT: DO I INSPIRE ACCOUNTABILITY?

Rate the statements in Parts A and B on the following 1–5 scale, being as honest as possible:

1 = Never 2 = Rarely 3 = Sometimes 4 = Usually 5 = Always

PART A

1. I rely on my employees to figure out how to handle issues that may arise with their tasks or projects. **1 2 3 4 5**

2. I rely on one or two individuals for the work that absolutely must get done, because I know these employees will always find a way to come through for me, no matter how full their plates are. **1 2 3 4 5**

3. "No excuses," "Just do it," or similar is a statement I have made to my employees. **1 2 3 4 5**

4. I've told my employees that they don't need to hear from me unless something has gone wrong. **1 2 3 4 5**

5. I believe that asking questions is a sign of incompetence. **1 2 3 4 5**

6. I resent team members or workers who take time off from work for family and personal reasons, or to "recharge." **1 2 3 4 5**

7. I believe a good employee instinctively performs to expectation even if the workload grows beyond what was originally anticipated or planned. **1 2 3 4 5**

8. I believe a good employee instinctively adapts to unforeseen changes in job description. **1 2 3 4 5**

9. I expect my team members to know which new assignments are most important or urgent and which should move lower on the to-do list. **1 2 3 4 5**

10. I spend at least 50 percent of my workweek "putting out fires" instead of attending to my own strategic or long-range planning tasks. **1 2 3 4 5**

11. I believe that my sole commitment to my employees is to pay them for the work I expect from them, and to provide the agreed-upon benefits. **1 2 3 4 5**

PART B

12. I reach out to teams and individuals, both formally and informally, to make sure I am aware of work and personal issues. **1 2 3 4 5**

13. I reach out to teams and individuals, both formally and informally, to get feedback regarding assignments. **1 2 3 4 5**

14. I reach out to teams and individuals, both formally and informally, to hear employees' expectations. **1 2 3 4 5**

15. I reach out to teams and individuals, both formally and informally, to hear employees' understanding of my own expectations. **1 2 3 4 5**

16. My employees readily and comfortably consult me and one another to keep company productivity and team morale levels high. **1 2 3 4 5**

17. My workers and I often express that we feel part of a greater whole or "family." **1 2 3 4 5**

18. Because I feel responsible for my employees' understanding of the work I am requesting, I respond promptly to requests for clarification. **1 2 3 4 5**

19. I run through employees' to-do lists with them before I assign new tasks and projects to let them know which tasks they can drop or delay, and which items can be delegated to other team members. **1 2 3 4 5**

20. I know that it is important to make it safe for people to push back and question such things as priorities, deadlines, and compensation, so I make a point of asking them for *any* questions or feedback they may have. **1 2 3 4 5**

21. If employees communicate that they are not able to carry out certain tasks/projects, I take action by either authorizing training, reassigning tasks to others with better aligned skill sets, or replacing the individual. **1 2 3 4 5**

22. Before problems arise, I let my employees know how they are doing in near real time via any or all of the following: ongoing feedback loops, scorecards, or scoreboards. **1 2 3 4 5**

KEY: Tally your scores for the two separate parts, A and B. Use your total points score and the following feedback as a guide to self-awareness work.

PART A:

1–11 points: You are sensitive to the needs of others and demonstrate a significant level of emotional intelligence (EQ), which may help to engage others and inspire them to their highest levels of performance (accountability).

12–23 points: You may at times be sensitive to the needs of others but need to better develop your emotional intelligence (EQ) to engage and inspire your employees to their highest level of performance (accountability).

24–35 points: To help your employees become more engaged and accountable and inspire them to their highest level of performance, you will need to develop significant levels of emotional intelligence (EQ).

36–47 points: Your emotional intelligence (EQ) levels are very low. You are actively preventing your employees from performing their jobs to their best ability, aligning their work with your own mission/vision and those of the company. You will need to work on enabling, empowering, and inspiring your people if you want them to achieve your shared goals.

47 points and above: You do not demonstrate emotional intelligence (EQ) in the workplace. On almost all fronts, you actively prevent your employees from performing their jobs to their best ability, aligning their work with your own mission/vision and those of the company. You need to undertake immediate efforts to enable,

empower, and inspire your people if you want them to achieve your shared goals.

PART B:

1-11 points: You have not allocated thought or planning to your own management ability to inspire account- ability in others. You are generally unaware that your own accountability to the enterprise includes enabling and empowering (as opposed to "holding") others to be accountable. To see measurable results, you need to develop the skills to inspire accountability,.

12-23 points: You have not allocated enough thought and planning to your own management ability to inspire accountability in others. You are somewhat aware of your own accountability to the enterprise, which includes enabling and empowering (as opposed to "holding") others to be accountable, but to see mea- surable results you need to better develop the skills to inspire accountability.

24-35 points: You have allocated some thought and planning to your own management ability to inspire accountability in others. You are aware of your own accountability to the enterprise, which includes enabling and empowering (as opposed to "holding") others to be accountable. To see better results, you need to ramp up your work on inspiring accountability.

36-47 points: You have allocated a good deal of thought and planning to your own management ability to inspire accountability in others. You have a keen sense of duty regarding your own accountability to the enterprise, which includes enabling and empowering (as opposed to "holding") others to be accountable. Additional work toward inspiring others will help to make you an outstanding business leader.

47 points and above: You readily and consistently inspire accountability and high performance among your workforce. Use and hone your top-flight leadership skills in this area to move your enterprise and its workforce to its highest levels of performance.

Now take a quick look at the telling exercise below, courtesy of Shannon Susko, adapted from her book *3HAG Way*.[7] The graph's simplicity can help you quickly locate your particular team accountability gremlins.

Team members are accountable for the team goal & leaders are coaching

Leaders are accountable team members are not

No team accountability

TEAM PERFORMANCE

ACCOUNTABILITY

---

7   Shannon Susko, *3HAG Way: The Strategic Execution System That Ensures Your Strategy Is Not a Wild-Ass Guess! (Whistler, BC: Ceozen Consulting, 2018).*

To use the graph above, estimate where your team lies in relation to the X and Y axes. The positioning indicates the following:

- **No team accountability.** No one is accountable for the team goal, not even the leaders. All teams and team members are siloed and focused on their department's or team's goals only, and are not concerned with the broader team goals.

- **Leaders are accountable, team members are not.** Leaders are aware and feel accountable for the whole company's team goal, but their team members are still focused on their individual and departmental goals.

- **Team members are accountable for the whole company's team goal, and their leaders are their coaches.** The whole company understands the team goal and is empowered, clear, and owning the team result. Leaders are there to guide and coach their team members for the win (the ultimate goal of team accountability).

THE 7CS FOR TWENTY-FIRST CENTURY SUCCESS

Whatever your results in the preceding assessment, a few things have undoubtedly become clear: your ability to enable, empower, and inspire your people to become more accountable is best achieved through *specific positive behaviors* on your part. You can begin to see that certain types of behaviors hold the greatest potential to trigger engagement and accountability among your executives and employees—and thus dramatically boost performance across the enterprise.

The flip side of this is that negative behaviors on your part can sabotage your end goal of facilitating a high-functioning organization. Those negative behaviors often are ingrained management behaviors that you may not be consciously aware of. Such actions keep you from getting what you need from your team members and workforce as a whole. They also prevent you from being accountable for your *own* mandate: inspiring others to be engaged in their workplace, enthusiastically contributing to the enterprise, and performing at their optimal levels.

So, *when employees fail to perform as expected, what's going on?*

As we've established, there are always internally logical reasons for human behavior—even when that behavior appears illogical from the outside looking in. Typically, when an employee fails to perform as expected, one or more of the following issues is behind that behavior. I call these factors the 7Cs:

- The **Culture** of the organization is preventing the employee from speaking his or her truth and telling the boss what is going on for him or her.

- There is a lack of **Clarity** about what is expected by when and at what standard of excellence, or about what the top priority is and what can wait until later.

- There is a lack of **Capacity** (manpower, resources, etc.) to do the job requested in the time frame requested.

- There is a lack of **Competence** on the part of the employee to do the requested task.

- There is a lack **Confidence** on the part of the employee to do the requested task.

- There is a lack of **Commitment** or caring on the part of the employee toward their boss or their company.

- The **Compensation** doesn't reward the desired behavior, and the employee may not feel motivated to be accountable.

Simply put, the 7Cs provide a clear and logical approach to the kind of inquiry a leader should engage in to surface the truth behind an employee's behavior. Only through this kind of methodical, targeted inquiry can a business leader know precisely what to do differently to motivate the desired behavior. The reality is, the responsibility for understanding and remedying all of the 7Cs rests with management. Think about it:

- If people don't tell you what's going on for them, who has created a **Culture** that discourages people from speaking their truth?

- If there is a lack of **Clarity**, who is responsible for ensuring clarity?

- If there is a lack of **Capacity**, who is responsible for ensuring adequate resources and time to complete a task?

- If there is a lack of **Competence**, who hired this person and failed to adequately train the employee for new assignments?

- If there is a lack of **Confidence**, who has failed to build the confidence of the employee?

- If there is a lack of **Commitment**, who has failed to engage the heart of the employee and make him or her feel appreciated?

- If there is a lack of **Compensation**, who has failed to create a compensation system that rewards the desired behaviors?

The bottom line? All of these problems can be dealt with by an effective leader who understands that it is the job of the *manager* to inspire accountability.

Importantly, the 7Cs method is designed to give twenty-first century managers the skills to attract, onboard, retain, and develop millennials (and succeeding generations) in the workplace. These young people will either be running with the company batons, working for the competition, or launching their own competing ventures. We need to inspire them to join our teams and help us raise our enterprises to new heights of success.

I created this straightforward 7Cs approach to help senior and mid-level managers quickly see results in themselves, their executives, and team leaders. The change can then expand like ripples on water, moving the entire organization to ever-widening levels of performance as the old model of ineffective command-and-control that *demands* accountability yields to the far more effective paradigm of inspiring accountability.

HOW TO INSPIRE ACCOUNTABILITY WITH THE 7CS

With the 7Cs you will learn to:

1. Create a **Culture** of safety for inquiry and two-way dialogue.

2. Promote **Clarity** instead of obscuring it.

3. Care about and better manage work **Capacity.**

4. Support and optimize **Competence** in the workplace.

5. Protect and develop job **Confidence** among employees.

6. Elicit **Commitment** by demonstrating your own commitment to your employees and showing that you care about them and their welfare.

7. Understand the impact of **Compensation** on motivation and behavior.

In brief, the 7Cs will serve as your no-fail "checklist" to help you quickly and effectively determine precisely why your people are falling short of accountability and thus blocking achievement of goals. From your 7Cs guidance, you'll know how you can inspire the results you need in specific areas. And because the 7Cs are often as interrelated as a carefully balanced ecosystem, a positive change in one "C" area tends to stabilize others. In fact, the 7Cs model can rewire the *collective management brain* for a dramatically improved employer/employee dynamic, robust enterprise culture, and a vastly more productive workplace.

Clients tell me that the invaluable C insights actually make timely intervention and course correction easy. Whether you're working with baby boomers or Gen Xers, or welcoming millennials into the fold, the 7Cs are your keys to inspiring the highest levels of accountability.

ACCOUNTABILITY FOLLOWS THE LEADER: YOU

In this new age of millennials, few company leaders and managers will effectively execute their company's vision and mission without understanding how to inspire accountability among their teams. The days of command-and-control ("Just do it!") have been breathing their last for some time now; just ask any boomer or Gen Xer who has recently moved on to more enlightened employment, leaving hopelessly disengaged colleagues behind. Even so, it has taken the mass disruption of the workplace by the incoming millennial generation to finally galvanize the attention this issue has long warranted.

TAKING ACTION: COMMIT TO FLIPPING YOUR MANAGEMENT PARADIGM

If you are ready to turn the page and change just about everything for the better by making changes in the way you manage others, check the following:

☐ Yes, I am willing to leave behind archaic management attitudes that for centuries have only generated struggles between bosses and workers.

☐ Yes, I am ready to resolve employee apathy and disengagement and drive remarkable improvement in enterprise performance.

☐ Yes, I am eager to attract and retain millennial workers, who will soon comprise the largest part of my workforce.

☐ Yes, I will be relieved to finally stop pleading, "Why can't people just do their jobs?"

CHAPTER TWO

MILLENNIALS, MANAGERS, AND ACCOUNTABILITY

A Gen Xer may be led to think their millennial employee is wasting the company's time and money, and ultimately underperforming, when she sees them constantly on their smartphone texting and talking to everyone in the office. In reality, the millennial's behavior was simply highly social and they were actually strategically gathering project-relevant information through the use of their extremely connected social network. In this example, what was perceived as a weakness was in fact a strength on the part of the younger generation. We have to see past the diverse set behaviors and instead focus on the outcomes we benefit from when we raise our [own] levels of accountability.

—Elizabeth Donahey, a California marketing director

Recently, one of my boomer clients confided, "I'm surrounded by these *kids* who seem to speak a different language and come from another world." She shook her head at me. "Every pop-culture reference they make in a meeting is one I either don't recognize or can't relate to. When I walk by offices and cubicles, people are tapping away on their keyboards and giggling, but no one else is nearby. I know they're all on social media, and it's making me nervous because I can't believe they're doing their work!"

"Are they getting things done?" I asked her.

"I suppose so," she responded, "but I can't tell if I'm giving them too much to do or not enough, and they keep lobbying me for more opportunities. They're so impatient!"

"Why not stretch their skills a bit, and see how they do?" I suggested.

"I'm certainly not going to give these people more responsibility, even though they keep telling me they're eager for it. I don't trust the results they're giving me right now! And why do they want to stop by my office and chat with me about everything? How am I supposed to get anything done?"

I started to speak, but she cut me off with "What's with this generation? And how can I put the fear of god into them like my bosses did with me?"

There's no disputing that the growing presence of the millennial generation in the workplace is presenting brand-new challenges in employee engagement and accountability. Yet, even before their millennial brethren arrived on the scene, boomers and Gen Xers have been struggling to stay engaged in the twenty-first century workplace. These earlier generations not only have endured company cultures with nineteenth and twentieth century "fear of god" mind-sets, but have held on as their organizations grappled with significant technological and cultural change. Today, overwhelmed by workplace demands and with many benefits, pensions, and other workplace incentives diminished, it is baby boomers who actually demonstrate the lowest level of engagement and the highest level of active disengagement of all the generations currently in the US workforce.[8] Gen Xers, with their pronounced preference for work/life balance and entrepreneurial pursuits, are right behind them.

MAKE WAY FOR MILLENNIALS

Still, it is the millennials, garnering press coverage everywhere, who are presenting a whole other challenge as they disrupt workplaces around the globe: many employers can't even get them *into* a conventional workplace, and if they do, millennials often won't stick.[9] Yet, as US millennials swell toward the 73 million mark in 2019,[10] they will overtake the boomers as America's largest generation. Their reticence to enter or remain in a traditional workplace where employers demand accountability presents a challenge of the greatest urgency.

Wall Street is discovering this right now. In fact, the bureaucratically entrenched financial sector is currently undergoing disruption that can only be termed volcanic as it scrambles to find a way to attract, retain, and actively engage a millennial workforce that will rise to positions of leadership by the time boomers retire. But decades, if not centuries, of management models must change to retain impatient hirelings who have no intention of "earning

---

8   In fact, nearly one in four boomers is actively disengaged: not able to perform his or her jobs, seeking employment elsewhere, negatively influencing fellow workers, and/or actively protesting working conditions online on websites such as Glassdoor, Indeed, or Vault. "There's a Generation Gap in Your Workplace," Gallup, August 6, 2013, https://news.gallup.com/businessjournal/163466/generation-gap-workplace.aspx.

9   Maurie Backman, "Why Millennials Resign Twice as Often as Older Workers," The Motley Fool, June 11, 2018, https://www.fool.com/careers/2018/06/11/why-millennials-resign-nearly-twice-as-often-as-ol.aspx.

10 Richard Fry, "Millennials projected to overtake Baby Boomers as America's largest generation," Pew Research Center, March 1, 2018, http://www.pewresearch.org/fact-tank/2018/03/01/millennials-overtake-baby-boomers/.

their dues" before they can make the world a better place for their companies and themselves.

Importantly, millennials look for meaning in their work. That meaning is described by *Forbes* as sharing their gifts, impacting the lives of others, and living their desired quality of life. Millennials like to share and receive feedback about their work and to work cross-functionally.[11] They do not unquestioningly follow autocratic rule. Millennials expect to have a relationship with their boss, and they seek managers whom they can regard as mentors. They are task- not time-oriented, are open to change, and believe regular office attendance is unnecessary: they measure work results by work completed, not time spent in an office. Perhaps because they've only known a world where technology obliterates the barriers between work and daily life, finding work/life balance is essential to millennials.

> DECADES, IF NOT CENTURIES, OF MANAGEMENT MODELS MUST CHANGE TO RETAIN IMPATIENT HIRELINGS WHO HAVE NO INTENTION OF "EARNING THEIR DUES" BEFORE THEY CAN MAKE THE WORLD A BETTER PLACE FOR THEIR COMPANIES AND THEMSELVES.

The millennial disruption is not an American or even a Western cultural phenomenon. Millennials are now exerting a huge influence on workforce behaviors all around the world. Managers in India, for instance, have been reporting the same employee accountability frustrations as have their counterparts in the United States, and

---

11   "Millennial Impact Reports," The Millennial Impact Report, 2017, http://www. themillennialimpact.com/.

probably for some time; after all, the work population in India currently contains 50 percent more millennials than in the US. Yet, for business leaders everywhere, the global reach of accountability issues does not make their own workplace challenges any less urgent. These employers still must figure out how to elicit accountability from their own workforces, because the impact of not doing so could be calamitous. The realization that "Just do your job!" has no teeth in this day and age should be a wake-up call. It must lead to a determination to find an effective route to achieving accountability in today's workplace—and find it soon.

KNOW YOUR MILLENNIAL WORKFORCE

Millennials have plenty to offer the twenty-first century workplace, and your company will reap the benefits with a greater understanding of what drives these innovative, enthusiastic employees. Below are characteristics you can exploit for the good of both company and employee. (You'll be using the 7Cs to adjust your own behavior patterns accordingly.)

- **Millennials have entitlement issues.** Yes, millennials do feel entitled to be taken seriously (they were raised that way), so follow their lead and dole out responsibility *up front*. It may take some time to change your old behavior patterns of withholding responsibility until it is "earned" (Boomer Motivation 101). But flipping this paradigm by offering clarity and support early will get results.

- **Millennials have confidence issues.** Although they were bred for success, millennials weren't nudged from the nest as their boomer parents were. Consequently, they are learning to stand on their own later than previous generations. That doesn't mean they won't be confident members of your workforce, or that initial signs of low confidence indicate reduced job capability. It means your support will get them up to speed more quickly than the blame game will. To develop enthusiastic and engaged millennial workers, drop the "toughen up" paradigm and give them the tools to serve you well.

- **Millennials don't push back; they just leave.** This may be the most difficult millennial characteristic to fathom, for *you* would do almost anything to keep your job when you were their age. But these young people travel light and are not daunted by temporary unemployment. They see no reason to suffer in an unfulfilling job when an exciting opportunity may be around the corner. The problem is, you won't know you've disengaged this worker until he is out the door. Creating a culture of safety where feedback is valued is essential if you want your millennials to remain on board and become enthusiastic, high-performing pros.

- **Millennials crave mentoring, because they've had parental guidance all their lives.** They're not trying to annoy you with their questions or need for further clarity; they are hoping you will help guide them so that they can do their best job for you. Seize this opportunity to help develop involved, committed workers who can bring much to the table and then go on to mentor others. Smart CEOs have taken advantage of this uniquely millennial trait by instituting company-wide "universities" where millennial employees are offered guidance and development. Such mentoring can help to create a workforce of engaged, accountable individuals who are loyal, innovative, and forward looking—just what the company's bottom line needs.

- **Millennials seek purpose.** Purpose seeking is one trait you can't easily instill, and here's a whole generation just brimming with the need to work with driving purpose. So make your company's mission your millennials' purpose. At the same time, be careful not to reduce your millennials' striving to a quest for the almighty dollar. That may have worked for previous dollar-driven generations, but these young people genuinely want to improve life for your customers, help to change the world with your product or services, or—best of all—contribute *new*, innovative ways to help your company make a difference in the world (the competitive edge you've been pursuing). Purpose seeking is millennial gold you can't afford to squander, so channel this invaluable trait wisely.

- **Millennials value empowerment over money.** This is not to say that millennials don't dream of their own billion-dollar start-ups; they do. But while they are within your walls, the responsibility and encouragement to contribute that you give them may greatly outweigh less significant monetary incentives. What millennials want is the ability to use their skills and talents to the utmost. Repressing their ability to contribute transmits to them that they are not valued. Take the time to evaluate their development and communicate with them regularly; your millennial hires have plenty to offer, even if you need to move them around to make the best use of their abilities. Too many managers are surprised to learn that the millennial they never got to know or appreciate went on to start up a dynamic organization—their competition.

TIP: Take a millennial to lunch (or corner one at your next cocktail party or sporting event). To manage others well, it helps to see management and company through their eyes. So, without grilling your millennial captive, ask questions such as "What was your biggest surprise when you entered the workplace?" "What have been the most difficult things to adapt to in the working world?" "What do you love/hate about your job?" The exercise may be easiest if the individual is not your employee, but even more revealing if they are.

MANAGING MILLENNIALS AND THEIR MANAGERS

Remember John, in Chapter One? The first day he came into my office, John bemoaned the fact that his people were not holding *their* people—now, largely millennials—accountable. The breakdown was preventing him from delivering to his boss the results that were expected of him. So I asked a simple question:

"What is your end goal?"

He looked at me as though I had a hearing problem. "What do you mean? I told you: I want results from my team, and with no excuses!"

"That's two separate goals," I pointed out. "Do you want results, or do you want no excuses? The reality is that you can have no excuses, but you may not get the results you want. But if what you really want is results, I can help you get results from your team, and I can even help your people get results from their people. But no one can guarantee you the results you need with 'no excuses.'"

At that moment, I was prepared for John to walk out the door. This was a man who was stretched very thin in his own post. His life at work was a kaleidoscope of never-ending meetings and demands that had only intensified as the workforce had gradually shifted toward twenty- and thirty-somethings—a demographic he and his reports were having a tough time managing. Like many senior-level managers, John's only hours to concentrate on his own backlog of work usually came right after dawn or the dinner hour. What's more, his work life (and its endless emails) routinely impinged upon such things as weekends, family time, and hoped-for vacations.

"I don't have any time to deal with excuses," he said flatly. "I have barely enough time to handle what I already have on my plate."

"What if you had more time on your plate because things were running smoothly, and people were doing their jobs better?" I asked him. "What if you did not have to spend a large part of every week putting out fires? What if you had more time for longer-range and strategic planning?"

"All right ..." he said, looking at me quizzically. "What do I have to do?"

"First," I said, "you have to be open to a paradigm shift in the way you have been thinking about accountability all these years." He thought for a moment and then agreed he would at least listen to what I had to say. "Second," I said, "You have to be open to changing some of your own behaviors in order to elicit the kinds of behaviors you want from others. Can you do that, or is your belief in your own approach—not currently working for you—so absolute that there is no room for change?"

"How complicated is this going to be?" he wanted to know.

I laughed. "It's not complicated at all," I assured him. "In fact, it will soon seem as logical as ABC. Especially C, and there are only seven of them."

COMMAND OR INSPIRE?

Before we could look at each of the 7Cs of accountability success, John first had to understand why relinquishing the current paradigm of demanding accountability in the workplace—the paradigm of holding others accountable—was so critical.

The challenge of accountability is, in essence, a performance challenge. After all, when workers fail to perform, what do their managers say? They say that the workers didn't do what was expected of them. Or, they didn't do it well enough or fast enough. Or, they didn't do it consistently. The employees committed to the task, but they didn't deliver.

Yet, a fundamental question can't be ignored: *When a boss tells an employee to do something and the employee responds, "Yes, boss," does that constitute agreement and thus commitment?*

When I visit workplaces to interview my clients' staffs about issues such as accountability, I often observe such interactions and note that after the unilateral command has been issued and the "Yes, boss" has been extracted, staffers often go back to their posts muttering, "Well, I'll never get that done," or, "Boy, that was a stupid idea." (And yes, I've learned to read lips over the years.)

The situation reminds me of parental directives to teenagers ("I told you to take out the trash! How many times do I have to tell you?") and how well such commands generally are received and carried out. The odds are definitely not with the house. On the other hand, when Billy knows that it is his job to do his homework and yet, time and again, he can't seem to get his math homework done, two reactions are common among parents:

A. A. Reprimand and/or penalize Billy for falling behind in his assignments.

B. B. Ask Billy where the problem lies.

The "B" conversation is pretty direct and usually starts like this: "Billy, is there something going on with the math homework situation?"

"I dunno." (Head down, staring at sneakers.)

"Billy, is there a reason you are not able to do your math homework?"

"I don't want to tell you, Dad."

"I want to help, Billy. Are you having trouble understanding the lessons and assignments? If that's the problem, we can fix that pretty easily with some extra instruction."

(Looking up from sneakers, hopeful.) "We can? That would be great, Dad. Then I could catch up!"

Parents who choose option A don't usually engage in a two-way conversation; they issue a reprimand, ultimatum, directive, or penalty. They get the satisfaction of letting their child know they simply will not tolerate poor performance in school or listen to excuses. They may have to mete out plenty of chastisement and revoke a series of privileges, but in the end they will have succeeded in generating a host of bad feelings (and dinner table acrimony) while their child's math performance falls further and further behind and the parent/child relationship continues to erode at the expense of family harmony.

Things are not much different in the workplace. The "I am holding you accountable" approach (A) claims to be results oriented, while the other tactic (B) actually is results oriented. Approach B also eliminates the circular, time-wasting dance of approach A that only serves to set off additional fires. (And new fires always need to be put out, which takes even more time away from a possible resolution toward better performance.)

Managers too often assume that because they have issued an order and have given a worker no choice but to swallow it, a mumbled "Yes" constitutes acceptance, and the staffer must figure out a way to deliver. In truth, without consent or opting in, the order is coercion. It not only feels like coercion to the recipient, but it stifles his or her opportunity to inform a manager of preventable obstacles or repercussions visible at the staffer's level. In the end, the one-way directive carries with it an outsized potential for failure, nonperformance, and nonaccountability.

TIP: Behavior in the workplace is often an extension of behavior in daily life. Think honestly about your interactions with spouses and children at home and with service individuals in daily life such as wait staff and salespeople: Do you have a pattern of *demanding* performance from them? Next time such an interaction presents itself, try saying instead, "I really need your help here. What can I do to help you help me? What would get us closer to a solution?" Then listen carefully to what they suggest, and try to act on the other person's request so that he or she can act on yours.

FORGING INQUIRY AND DIALOGUE

There's a very good reason why the current paradigm of "holding one accountable" is ultimately unworkable: while it provides a wide-open communication pathway for the *manager's* message, it effectively shuts down the flow of communication in the opposite direction, to the manager, preventing the manager from receiving the most valuable information possible: the root cause of the roadblock in the critical work process.

To enlightened managers, this bit of information from an individual closer to the task is gold. It forges a direct route to the optimal completion of the task. Workers who feel safe to offer feedback or questions can identify current obstacles and, because they are closest to the challenge at hand, frequently have on-point, time-saving suggestions to effect process change going forward. "No excuses!" and similar directives like "Just make it happen!" may feel like time-savers to an already overextended manager, but in reality they shut down the vital two-way flow of communication, often make accountability impossible, and can result in additional project roadblocks (fires), not to mention employee disengagement (which generates its own constellation of negative by-products).

Then too, because only limited direction is offered with directives and because the tone of voice suggests "Do it immediately—

drop everything to get this done," staffers run off in new directions, ejecting or back-burnering tasks in which they were already engaged. The sense is that there are no priorities, while at the same time everything is a priority. Yet, effective execution relies on a manager's ability to help his or her people prioritize and re-prioritize effectively, even on the fly. What you don't want to see is your people spending 80 percent of their time on the 20 percent of tasks that are (a) least important but easiest to knock off the list or (b) the last to be added to it.

Rich, a division vice president employed by a fast-growing cloud security firm, recently told me, "Every time we have a security problem, it's urgent and important! My team and I live in crisis mode twenty-four seven because we're understaffed, and training is not keeping up with the changing technology. We desperately need at least two new hires with an assortment of the skills we're lacking, plus the dollars for ongoing training for the whole unit."

Unfortunately, his senior vice president's attitude was "We're not spending money on that right now; just get the work done." But how could that reaction possibly contribute to a solution that would alleviate the problem and benefit the unit, the division, and the enterprise as a whole? The answer is, it couldn't. It only served to shut down the two-way flow of information so crucial to brainstorming, innovation, and resolution.

After I worked with Rich and we brought in his senior vice president, a reciprocal dialogue was opened to explore a way to alleviate the twenty-four-seven crisis environment and keep the existing talent from jumping ship. Both Rich and his senior vice president took the time to ask thoughtful questions, and they each listened carefully to what the other had to say. "Shut down" tactics were not permitted within this conversation; the goal was to find a solution even if it was not the perfect solution. The ramifications of not responding to the seriousness of the situation were finally presented in detail and discussed.

In the end, Rich succeeded in receiving budget approval for one new hire, which was certainly an improvement on "I don't want to hear it." In addition, a team member was designated as training lead, and she quickly introduced some creative and cost-effective training measures that were put in place to help get the unit up to speed on new skills. The two vice presidents are also reassessing the unit's prioritization scheme, to make sure a clearly communicated triage plan is firmly in place. Most importantly, both the vice president and his senior vice president are making a concerted effort to keep the flow of inquiry and dialogue running between them and among all unit members, so that situations do not automatically escalate to crises as they had previously. The two vice presidents are relying on the 7Cs and the many tools and techniques they learned in coaching to help them. Still, it's hard not to wonder how many calamities might have been averted or quickly resolved earlier on by first opening a process of inquiry and two-way dialogue.

CHANGE MANAGEMENT ATTITUDES *FIRST*

One glance at current marketplace winners and losers makes it crystal clear that if businesses are to thrive or even remain viable, management attitudes must change and change now. According to the Good Media Group,[12] which partners with the likes of Google, Starbucks, and L'Oréal, today's workforce wants to be "excited to get out of bed" each morning, and work at "a place that inspires us to make our own company better." Good's employees should know: their millennial

---

12   www.good.is

and other demographics represent what yours will be by 2020 if they aren't already.

To help US and global managers better grasp the kind of attitudinal change that really pays off, Good has selected "30 Places We Want to Work"—a list that comprises organizations large and small, venerable and start-up, profit and nonprofit. Whole Foods, Seventh Generation, Toms, Etsy, Patagonia, Kickstarter, and Trader Joe's made the list,[13] as did TED, Amalgamated Bank, John S. and James L. Knight Foundation, Wieden+Kennedy, DonorsChoose, Acumen, and Zipcar. Right now, says the Good website, companies known for their good practices and treatment of employees are "rare and commendable."

But they won't be rare for long, as more and more organizations take to heart the importance of changing management attitudes from those of "being inflexible, making things difficult, being quick to blame and punish employees, not showing that they care about their workers, and not recognizing accomplishments," says Brigette Hyacinth, bestselling author of *The Future of Leadership: Rise of Automation, Robotics and Artificial Intelligence*.[14]

Frankly, people don't leave their companies as much as they leave their bosses. In fact, at some point in their career, one in two employees has left a job to get away from a manager. No surprise, as only 18 percent of current managers have the "high talent (that unique combination of talents needed to help a team achieve excellence in a way that significantly improves a company's performance)"[15]

---

13   "30 Places We Want to Work," Good Media Group, November 11, 2010, https://www.good.is/slideshows/30-places-we-want-to-work.

14   Brigette Hyacinth, *The Future of Leadership: Rise of Automation, Robotics and Artificial Intelligence (MBA Caribbean Organisation, October 6, 2017)*.

15   "State of the American Manager," Gallup, April 2015, https://www.gallup.com/services/182138/state-american-manager.aspx.

for which they were hired. But employees who have great managers clearly drive better financial performance for companies.[16]

Simply put, to change workers' attitudes about their own accountability in the workplace, it is imperative to change *management attitudes first.*

TAKING ACTION: THINK BACK ABOUT YOUR OWN JOBS AND MANAGERS

Responding to the questions and suggestions below is a good way to quickly reconnect with yourself as an employee under an uninspiring (or worse) manager. How effective did you believe your bosses' management styles were? Ask yourself:

- ☐ Did you ever leave a job because of your discomfort working for your boss?

- ☐ If so, on how many occasions?

- ☐ If not, did you ever *wish* you could leave your job because of your discomfort working for your boss?

- ☐ Try to review your career objectively and list the number of occasions you would have left if you could.

---

16 Andrew Chamberlain, "6 Studies Showing Satisfied Employees Drive Business Results," Glassdoor, December 5, 2017, https://www.glassdoor.com/research/satisfied-employees-drive-business-results/.

☐ Then, review in your mind what became of those working relationships or your tenure at those companies, to gauge the effect of your own disengagement.

CHAPTER THREE

SAILING THE 7CS TO ACCOUNTABILITY

I never learn anything talking. I only learn things when I ask questions.

**—Lou Holz, former American football player,
coach, and oftentimes controversial analyst**

On Monday morning, Matthew's boss Charlene called him into her office to announce that she was handing off an important project that would require the attention of Matthew and two of his team members. Completion deadline: Friday.

"You got this covered?" Charlene asked him as she turned her attention to a call coming in at that moment.

"No problem," Matthew assured her. Noting her hand signal to close the door behind him, he started for his own office. With a new surge of stress closing in on him, he momentarily panicked until he thought of Jake and Sarah, his two team members who had the expertise to handle the job, which the three of them would be managing off-site for a major client. Matthew breathed a sigh of relief and, back in his own office, called in the two others to lay out the details Charlene had given him. The three of them would have to figure out the rest as they dove in.

57

All went fairly well until early Thursday morning, when Sarah reached Matthew at home just before he was to leave for the client's site. She informed him that she had been in a car accident the night before and was stuck at the hospital with a ruptured spleen. After a moment to mentally grapple with the curveball, he wished her a speedy recovery and told her not to worry about work. Then he grabbed his files and charged out the door. He'd have to call Charlene from the road and tell her the bad news. He dreaded the conversation but could only hope that she would tell him not to panic while together they performed some serious troubleshooting. Charlene had to know he would do anything he could, but he did need her input to proceed.

A few moments later, he delivered the news of the setback. "I'm stuck without one of my key resources," he explained. "Can we talk about how best to handle this so that we keep the client happy?" he asked her.

"You figure it out!" Charlene barked at him. "Get it done. I don't want excuses!"

In the end, while the clock was ticking toward Friday, Matthew queried a series of department heads to see if he could find someone suitable to take Sarah's place. The individual he located came into the project late with limited background and struggled to help Matthew and Jake serve the client as promised. When the project was finalized the following Monday instead of Friday, Charlene was furious and told Matthew she could not understand why he had not handled the situation as she would have done. Matthew held his tongue instead of pointing out that he had no way of knowing what she would have done, since she had not shared that information with him when he needed it.

Two weeks after Charlene admonished Matthew, his semiannual review reflected her dissatisfaction with his performance. Matthew later admitted that he couldn't get over his frustration at not being able to elicit guidance from his manager when he needed it most. He said nothing to anyone, but as he looked around his organization, he realized that the "no excuses" mantra was a way of life there, and he suddenly understood that he would never be able to ask questions or get the information he needed without appearing incompetent.

One day a few weeks later, Matthew handed in his resignation with no real explanation. Charlene was truly surprised, for she felt he was bright and showed promise. He was the third new team member she had lost in eighteen months, and she was starting to suspect that his generation of millennials just wasn't cut out for the business world. She wondered if she might have to go through quite a number of Matthews before she found someone she could depend on to deliver results.

How do I know about this story? I was called in to coach Charlene, a top executive in the company, who was having issues retaining her millennial hires. In the process of my coaching engagement, among other tools and tactics I employed to clarify the picture, I conducted a 360-degree assessment, confidentially meeting with and interviewing Charlene's colleagues and reports. In that way, I could piece together situations like the one with Matthew and better help Charlene to see how her own behavior was impacting her team, the organization, and her own career path.

Working closely together, Charlene and I attacked the first C of Culture—specifically, the "no excuses" culture that she (and so many other top-level managers) unwittingly foster. Charlene soon saw that such a culture not only makes it impossible for millennials to remain engaged and accountable, it makes it virtually impossible for *anyone* to succeed in an environment where they cannot safely question, discuss, clarify, and engage.

Charlene and I continued our coaching engagement, navigating the 7Cs a good deal more easily than she may have initially imagined. Months later, when we spoke again, she reported that she was no longer struggling with her millennial hires. In fact, she found that with an open, ongoing reciprocal dialogue as part of the working culture, her millennials were helping to teach *her* about all the new things the young generation of workers could bring to the table that would greatly benefit her area and the company as a whole.

As for Matthew, he traveled for a couple of months and returned with a novel business plan for a start-up. He funded it with angel money from his parents and a number of relatives. Then he used the skills and business acumen he had learned during his time working under Charlene to find and serve his first clients. It seems Charlene's original assessment was correct: Matthew was pretty smart after all.

THE 7CS PROMPT YOU TO DO YOUR GROUNDWORK

Charlene and so many others I have coached learn that, in the most important aspects of working life, the comparatively small amount of time spent up front laying the foundation for the challenges ahead ensures greater achievement of goals. But there's more to the equation: that time will also save you—the manager—countless hours, days, and weeks on the *back end*, where you would ordinarily be scrambling to put out fires, revise and retool, and patch, patch, patch.

Time allocated for inquiry, listening, and engagement will also serve to build and solidify relationships with your people, rewarding you with higher levels of team engagement, loyalty, and performance all along the way. And—no small benefit—the time you spend up front to ensure that your team's projects succeed will free you for the longer-range visualizing, planning, and innovation that will bring you satisfaction, achievement, and recognition in your own career path.

THE 7CS ENSURE AN OUTCOME ORIENTATION

Many of my clients tell me that one of the aspects of the 7Cs they value most is that they help them highlight the difference between goal-oriented behavior specifically designed to achieve desired outcomes and unproductive patterns of behavior that persisted for no better reason than that they had been inherited. I couldn't have said it better.

In fact, we know from its long history of failure that "slave-driving" behavior does not result in desired outcomes. Sure, by beating others with a stick you may initially get some results, but sooner or later coercion backfires, just as it did with Charlene and Matthew. In the workplace, that kind of backfiring translates into apathy, widespread disengagement, and active disengagement wherein workers find all sorts of ingenious, passive-aggressive ways to rebel at the company's expense. (Matthew rebelled in an even more straightforward way: he quit and then launched his own company.)

One should never underestimate the power of under-the-radar insurgency, however; it is one of the reasons that Glassdoor attracts so many views every day. On Glassdoor, Vault, and other websites like them, disgruntled workers finally get their chance to speak up and speak *out*, providing invaluable insight to job candidates everywhere and making it nearly impossible for a targeted company to attract and retain top talent, the lifeblood of any business.

But progressing through the 7Cs is its own reward, as first management and then workforce attitudes and behavior patterns change. This effectively flips the slave-driver paradigm into one of inspired accountability, wherein the workforce supports and furthers the company mission as employees' personal missions of satisfaction in the workplace are achieved.

TRACE YOUR MANAGEMENT STYLE ROOTS

Is your management style outcome oriented or inherited? Answer the following five questions and consider the impact on (a) your present management style, (b) the management style of your direct reports, and (c) the culture of your organization.

1. Who was your own management mentor, and approximately which year(s) did you work for this individual?

2. What was his or her management style?

3. Was your mentor's management style representative of the organization's culture?

4. Did you ever consider quitting specifically because of your mentor's management style or the management culture of the organization?

5. Has your own management style changed in recent years? If so, how and why?

6. Do you think your management style has been a conscious choice or an inheritance?

THE 7CS PROVIDE A SECURE FRAMEWORK FOR INQUIRY AND DIALOGUE

It can't be stressed enough: the most outstanding company leaders I know have, throughout their careers, relied on inquiry and reciprocal dialogue with their reports to make sure their people have access to whatever they need to keep their companies on "best" lists everywhere.

"Would it help to review this week's priorities with me?" and "Can your current workload accommodate this new project?" are questions these managers ask without a second thought. It is the way such leaders demonstrate their desire to connect with their people and exchange information to further the joint mission. The 7Cs *ensure* a secure framework for just this type of inquiry. And it is inquiry that most effectively opens the door to two-way (reciprocal) dialogue.

Two-way dialogue is so valuable because it is the ongoing exchange of information that ensures that work progresses smoothly with limited surprises, fewer fires to put out, reduced misunderstanding, and greatly increased goodwill and engagement across the enterprise. Not only are goals achieved, but greater numbers of goals become accessible more quickly, resulting in a nimble and high-performing workplace.

THE 7CS CONNECT HEAD, HEART, AND GUT

At Southwest Airlines, consistently ranked high in both customer *and* employee satisfaction, managers know where their priorities lie: *with the employees.* The logic here is simple, and tantamount to the old "If mama ain't happy, ain't no one happy" maxim: engaged and enthusiastic employees treat customers well, and delighted customers come back—which makes for very happy shareholders. The airline hires employees who want to take initiative and be actively engaged in the success of their company. To that end, managers encourage their staffers to speak up and take responsibility (be accountable) for the success of the company. The Southwest culture is an open one where every worker has a voice, and no one is shut down. Since 2010, when Glassdoor named Southwest the number one Best Place to Work, the airline has made Glassdoor's Top 50 list every year. Southwest managers focus on the front end—what their employees need to do their jobs—and everyone reaps the benefits.

Employers like Southwest Airlines understand that accountability necessitates an appeal to the "head, heart, and gut" of its employees. They know that the *head* needs to be excited by the mission, vision, and values of the company. The *heart* needs to care about the team, the manager, and the company because it has been inspired to do so. And the *gut* needs to be motivated by the belief that "our goal can be accomplished and *I* can do it."

Yet, the "head, heart, gut" engagement (and the resulting accountability) that managers need to inspire cannot come about without first looking at and changing entrenched management attitudes—flipping the paradigm of holding others accountable. The largest part of that work is made possible by creating a culture where employees feel safe and welcome to contribute, as they do at Southwest Airlines and other enlightened enterprises.

According to HR and corporate leadership analyst Josh Bersin, companies that are voted Best Places to Work appreciate the concept of head, heart, and gut. Bersin says that they "don't just have Ping-Pong tables and free lunch, they have a 'soul' that makes work exciting and energizing. They invest in great management and leadership. They train and develop people so that they can grow. And they define their business in a way that brings meaning and purpose to the organization."[17]

TIP: Uh oh, what do people think? Companies like Google and Boston Consulting Group engage and retain their employees (and land on the Best Places to Work lists every year). One way they achieve that is by surveying their employees to make *sure* they know what their people are thinking. In that way, the company can consistently support success for employees, their company's leadership, and their enterprise as a whole. Are you open to surveying your people to see what they think about their jobs, the company, and their leader (you)? If the idea doesn't thrill you, ask yourself the following questions, and write down your responses for frequent reference:

---

17   Josh Bersin, "Why Companies Fail to Engage Today's Workforce: The Over-whelmed Employee," *Forbes*, March 15, 2014, https://www.forbes.com/sites/joshbersin/2014/03/15/why-companies-fail-to-engage-todays-workforce-the-overwhelmed-employee/#3bba7d844726.

- What specifically makes me uneasy about such a survey?
- What would I hope not to hear?

Your answers are clues to existing obstacles to accountability, which you will need to address.

THE 7CS BUILD "A-PLAYERS"

Companies like Salesforce, Google, and Boston Consulting Group are teeming with "A-player" employees. How do they do it? After all, *every* manager wants A-player employees—those individuals who are so good at what they do, so self-motivated and accountable, that they barely need to be managed at all.

The secret is that at every company/employee juncture—attracting, hiring, casting roles, creating company culture, mentoring, supporting, training, promoting—the companies above and others like them listen to their employees to uncover what those employees need in order to succeed. What's more, Best Places to Work do not wait to be alerted to need by their employees; smart leadership and managers actively solicit that information through inquiry. They inspire reciprocal conversations that give them all the golden information they require to ensure their people can become A-players whose work is fully aligned with the mission and vision of the company.

There is nothing mysterious about A-players. They are people with jobs and careers they love, careers that reward them in any number of ways. A-player *companies* take that love all the way to the bank—and they should: they helped to develop their employees' passion to create outstanding products and services.

As for A-player managers, they know that it's their job to find and nurture A-players. A-player managers:

- Are good listeners and good interviewers; they help their people communicate the information they must have in order to help everyone succeed.

- Are respectful and live the tenets of a strong company culture that fosters integrity and trust.

- Encourage their people to take risks, even if they fail; they see failures as necessary to forward movement, and fear of failure as an obstacle to progress and innovation.

In a safe and nurturing culture, here's what an honest and open assignment discussion between an A-player manager and an A-player employee might sound like:

Megan: "Rob, do you have any questions about the work I just described?"

Rob: "I do. I can get this done for you, but the job is actually out of my skill set, and I just hate working with those programs. Could you give that to someone else? I'll be happy to help you with that Jones project instead; I've been thinking about it and I've got some great ideas for it. I'd like to see if you're willing to take a chance on them."

Megan: "Yes, I can talk to Serena about the program work—she's good at that stuff. Let's meet at 11:30 and go over the Jones project. I had no idea you could work on that, and I'd love to hear your ideas."

Here's what another important work discussion between a manager and employee might sound like in an A-player culture, where managers who strive to retain their valuable employees *need to know what their employees think and need:*

Brandon: "Katie, I need you to work late again tonight. I know you've worked late hours all this month, but this workload is not letting up."

Katie: "Brandon, I understand that we're slammed these days, but I have two young kids who have ballet recitals and sports meets, and I'm not willing to miss their important life events as they're growing up. Can we meet in a few minutes and discuss how we might be able to staff up this position adequately so that I can do a good job for you without sacrificing my family life? I'm sure that together we can find a solution."

CHAPTER FOUR

CREATING A CULTURE OF SAFETY FOR INQUIRY AND TWO-WAY DIALOGUE

Why is culture so important to a business? Here is a simple way to frame it. The stronger the culture, the less corporate process a company needs. When the culture is strong, you can trust everyone to do the right thing.

—Brian Chesky, CEO and cofounder of Airbnb

In the preceding chapter, the story of Matthew and his boss Charlene was an important look at an unenlightened manager losing her millennial hires in a competitive marketplace. Charlene certainly needed to flip her management paradigm and gain a clear understanding of how the 7Cs could dramatically change her management style and bring employee accountability back to the table. But the story of Matthew and Charlene is also a powerful introduction to this chapter on creating a culture of safety. To wit:

Two weeks after Charlene admonished Matthew, his semiannual review reflected her dissatisfaction with his performance. Matthew later admitted that he couldn't get over his frustration at not being able to elicit guidance from his manager when he needed it most. He said nothing to anyone, *but as he looked around his organization, he realized that the "no excuses" mantra was a way of life there, and he suddenly understood that he would never be able to ask questions or get the information he needed without appearing incompetent.*

Evidently, Charlene had not been the only manager in her organization who was perpetuating a "no excuses" culture. Feeding and sustaining nonaccountability had grown to be a widespread culture throughout the company, and all the company's employees came to know that.

NO EXCUSES VS. NO SURPRISES

Today, for so many reasons (speed of change, being stretched too thin, flattening of organizations, operating lean), business leaders and managers at all levels are under a great deal of pressure to get more and more done in less and less time. Yet, the conspicuous difference between demanding "no excuses" and wanting "no surprises" is something to seriously consider.

A culture that demands "no excuses" is one that makes it highly risky to ask for feedback, direction, or guidance. On the other hand, a culture that encourages "no surprises" is one in which all constituents routinely *solicit* and readily *provide* information early on, within any and every process possible, to dramatically reduce the potential for surprises—otherwise known as *stuff going wrong.*

Cultures that work toward zero surprises are also those that have proven the time- and glitch-saving value of the two-way dialogue. By urging the company managers to institute two-way dialogue with their employees through purposeful inquiry ("Is your department adequately staffed to handle this new client?" as opposed to the more ambiguous "Got it covered?"), a culture of safety is demonstrated. Workers feel encouraged to always make certain that they have what they need to perform at the highest levels, in full alignment with company mission and vision.

Top managers have known for some time that there is safety in ensuring that goals are well-thought-out SMART goals.[18] Likewise, there is the assurance of safety in the 7Cs. First and foremost, it resides in the C of Culture: the creation of a *safe* culture. In fact, it is the creation of a safe culture that impacts each and every C to follow: Clarity, Capacity, Competence, Confidence, Commitment, and Compensation. Importantly, *no business leader can effectively use the 7Cs checklist to pinpoint accountability obstacles unless a safe environment for inquiry and two-way dialogue exists first.*

So, ask yourself the obvious question: Do you *want* to hear the truth about the work at hand? Do you *want* to know what the problems-to-come may be?

TIP: Connect the dots to a safer culture. First, estimate what percentage of the time your people do what you expect them to do. Now, estimate the percentage of the time you assign work and also run through a thoughtful process of inquiry with your employee(s) regarding the assignment,

---

18   SMART goals refer to the mnemonic acronym for setting objectives in project management, employee-performance management, and personal development. The letters generally stand for Specific, Measurable, Achievable, Relevant, and Time-bound. SMART goals should be clearly and thoughtfully defined prior to action.

to encourage questions and the exchange of information before work begins.

Estimates usually mirror each other. For example, "People here can only do their jobs well or be accountable for their mistakes about 25 percent of the time (so I churn through a lot of employees)." Another example estimate is: "Two-way conversations about assignments happen only about 25 percent of the time (I expect people to do their work without asking a million questions)." If both estimates are low, you will need to work on creating a safer culture.

BUILD A WINNING CULTURE

Many years ago, I worked with the leadership team of ConAgra Foods, a multibillion-dollar food conglomerate that had been struggling with disengagement and thus accountability issues. The company had recently hired a new CEO, who quickly came to see that the huge enterprise with offices throughout the Midwest was plagued by culture issues. The culture did not encourage enthusiastic employee participation in work via an ethos of inquiry and dialogue. When the new CEO arrived, the company motto was pretty much "If you don't work on Saturday, don't even bother to come in on Monday." The culture was one of "No news is good news," where the only news that employees routinely received was criticism.

This new CEO saw at once that toxic cultural issues had had a huge systemic impact. He understood that an initiative to completely revamp the company culture could take years, not months, but he forged ahead full throttle, knowing that a solid culture would, in the end, undergird every single thing he hoped to accomplish, to position the company well in the years ahead. These were his steps:

- **Step One:** to determine the core values that would constitute a safe and productive culture in which all would thrive, to the *mutual benefit of the business and the workers.*

- **Step Two:** to communicate the culture at every possible opportunity so that every single employee would have no doubt whatsoever what the company stood for, what the expectations were, and how welcome each individual's participation was.

- **Step Three:** to institute behavioral change through every method possible, and then keep at it.

- **Step Four:** to ensure that everyone throughout the organization "lived" the core values and operated within the culture of the company. The values trickled down from the very top of the organizational chart; no lip service was acceptable.

- **Step Five:** to provide coaching for executives at all levels of the organization, beginning with division presidents and cascading down through the ranks. I was part of a team that worked with executives at this company over a four-year period to bring about culture change.

One of his tools to accomplish this may sound simplistic, but to this day I clearly recall the underground passageway walls that led to the company cafeteria. On those walls, the core values of the company were painted in large wording for all to see. As they walked to and from the communal gathering place, no manager, worker, or visitor could spend even one day on site without being reminded of the strong culture supporting and embracing all endeavors.

The leader of this mammoth enterprise understood that culture is not just about connecting employees to one another. It is all about what is valued, rewarded, and reinforced throughout the organization by every manager, from the CEO on down.

TIP: Try this "ten dimes" behavioral-change exercise practiced by a visionary CEO. To change your habit of criticizing instead of motivating, put ten dimes in your left pocket every day. Each time you catch an employee doing something right and compliment him or her for it in a sincere way, move one dime into your right pocket. Your goal is to move ten dimes every day.

BEST PRACTICES: CULTURES THAT WIN

How do corporations that head up the various "best companies" lists provide safe cultures in which employees thrive and thus are engaged and accountable for their work? Some Best Places to Work, like the fast-growing digital analytics company InfoTrust (ranked at the top of *Inc.* magazine's list in 2017), strive to provide perks and benefits. InfoTrust, for one, provides employee and family insurance, meets all daily food needs, and offers paid supplemental education and training, all to ensure that employees can laser-focus on the company's mission. "Our goal is to remove all life friction so our people can focus while they're at work," InfoTrust CEO Alex Yastrebenetsky confirmed to *Inc.*[19]

Yet there's so much more to creating a winning business culture, insist leaders of "best" workplaces. In 2017, for instance, InfoTrust laid out its three-year "Vivid Vision" for worldwide employees during a week of training, fun events, and team building at the corporate headquarters, designed to inspire employees to live the company's core values. The clearly communicated "short and focused" Vivid Vision document, says Yastrebenetsky, ensures that everyone—CEO, partners, investors, and employees—are aligned for success.

SALESFORCE

In the number one spot on both *Fortune* and Indeed's "best" 2018 list is Salesforce, a Fortune 500 company and the world's fourth largest software concern, with over thirty thousand global employees across twenty-five countries. No small thing in this day and age, Salesforce also consistently ranks at the top of *Fortune*'s "100 Best Workplaces for Millennials" list.

According to president and chief people officer Cindy Robbins,[20] "The fact that we have been able to stay on the *Fortune* list for a decade—and move up to the number one spot—is a true testament to our unwavering commitment to our people and our intentional approach to our culture." She adds: "We inspire each other and the industry through our values of trust, growth, innovation, and

---

19   Benjamin P. Hardy, "Want an Amazing Organizational Culture? Here's Some Tips from One of the Best," *Inc., May 24, 2018,* https://www.inc.com/benjamin-p-hardy/want-an-amazing-organizational-culture-heres-some-tips-from-one-of-best.html.

20   Cindy Robbins, "Salesforce Is #1 on the Fortune '100 Best Companies to Work For," Salesforce, February 15, 2018, https://www.salesforce.com/blog/2018/02/salesforce-fortune-100-best-companies-to-work.

equality. We believe culture is the key to our ability to attract and retain the best employees and the world's leading brands, and to our capability to drive change in our communities."

There are myriad ways Salesforce creates a safe culture of trust and employee inspiration. One essential way is via tools that enhance the ongoing two-way dialogue with its employees. In this way, company managers can consistently hear their employees' "truth" and better understand their relationship with and perception of the company. Among those tools:

- **Salesforce gives employees a hashtag to share their experiences** with the culture-in-action on their social networks. (The Salesforce hashtag is #SalesforceOhana—check it out.)

- **Salesforce consistently encourages employees to share their experiences of the Salesforce culture on employer review sites.** (Could *your* company confidently send your employees to CareerBliss, Comparably, or Indeed?)

- **Salesforce urges employees to share their stories and tips on how to bring company values to life** on the company culture blog (or other company blogs) or in the employee community.

- **Salesforce conducts regular and frequent employee surveys, posing questions** regarding how well employees think the company is doing in living its values. Recent questions and survey feedback include:

    □ "Imagine a top sales associate who, time after time, demonstrates a lack of integrity, which is one of your core values. Do you consider letting her go?"

- □ "What about promoting a successful customer service representative who is consistently disrespectful to others? Do you keep him on board?"

- □ "Even if there's a negative financial impact on the business, if you are serious about your values, you'll make those tough decisions. You'll put your culture and your people first, and others will notice."

- **Salesforce's most effective safe-culture tool: "Act on the feedback!"**

GOOGLE

In 2018, the employee review website Comparably named Google the tech company with the best corporate culture, and no one was surprised. Sure, Google's Silicon Valley campus and the company's perks (designed to help workers focus on their work challenges without distractions) have been groundbreakers. But according to the Forbes Technology Council, much of the Comparably award recognition had to do with something else: the creation of a culture that makes it *safe* to succeed—brilliantly. To the Google mind-set, safety is all about creating a strong relationship between managers and their charges.

"Google embraces the most important element of an employer-employee relationship: trust," one Council member stated. "Google's willingness to trust their employees is what breeds creativity, above-and-beyond performance and job satisfaction. We should all take a page from their book." Said another: "It's the way management and teammates treat one another. That's what truly matters at the end of the day."[21]

BOSTON CONSULTING GROUP

And at Boston Consulting Group (BCG), which for eight consecutive years has been recognized as one of the *Fortune* "Best Companies to Work For" (and has ranked in the top dozen since 2006), leadership knows it is their priority to *personally* help employees succeed. Even junior staffers report that they feel they have access to leadership worldwide. BCG accountability thrives with the support of well-established and engaged employee resource networks. The company also has launched numerous networks and initiatives specifically designed to connect people across the organization, so that everyone can get help and guidance when they need it. Most importantly, a culture of safety and trust exists because, as an astounding 98 percent of BCG employees report, "Management is honest and ethical in its business practices."[22] Not surprisingly, BCG leadership models *outside* the organization what it practices and expects *inside* the organization, too.

WHAT HAPPENS WITHOUT CORE VALUES?

Not long ago, I worked with two owners of a real estate concern who were brothers. The brothers had four large offices and wanted to

---

21   Forbes Technology Council, "13 Reasons Google Deserves Its 'Best Company Culture' Award," *Forbes, February 8, 2018,* https://www.forbes.com/sites/forbestechcouncil/2018/02/08/13-reasons-google-deserves-its-best-company-culture-award/.

22   "BCG Continues to be Named Premier Employer and Ranks Near Top of Fortune's '100 Best Companies to Work For' List for a Fifth Straight Year," BCG, February 15, 2018, https://www.bcg.com/perspectives/184567.

keep expanding, but they had developed serious issues holding onto agents. One of the brothers, Bob, worked behind the scenes in the corporation as the CFO; the other, Sid, was the CEO and the face of the company. Sid interacted with his senior managers, staff, and agents on a daily basis.

At the urging of his brother, Sid came to me for executive coaching. There had been employee feedback indicating there was a disconnect between the espoused core values of the business and faithfulness to those values. Sid's people simply didn't feel that their CEO lived the core value of integrity to which he constantly gave lip service.

"Integrity is what sets us apart from our competition," Sid always told his customers and employees. "We stand behind our word!" In real estate, Sid explained to all, an agent's word is his or her bond. He expected total integrity from his agents, staff, and all employees, he told anyone who would listen. He would not stand for anything less.

The problem was, Sid had no integrity whatsoever. What's more (as I discovered through a confidential survey of all staff members, and follow-up interviews), everyone knew it. Consequently, the company's culture was entirely disconnected from the espoused cultural values. When I spent time with his people, confidentially querying them about the issues at hand, they revealed that Sid was an extraordinarily self-focused individual who did precisely as he pleased, consistently operating in his own self-interest, often at the expense of others. He would routinely make promises and then go back on them. He would say one thing and then do something else entirely. He made it clear to all that he reserved the right to change his mind (often in nanoseconds). No one knew where they stood with him, and no one could trust him. In effect, Sid's mantra was: "Integrity is our core value, but *I* don't have to have integrity; I can do whatever I want." Not surprisingly, his people learned to model the core values that Sid actually lived, not espoused. They, too, did what they wanted, often to the detriment of the company. And then they left for more attractive situations.

EVERY ORGANIZATION HAS CORE VALUES THAT FORM THE BASIS FOR THE COMPANY CULTURE AND GOVERN WHAT GETS REWARDED.

Sid never made headway with his coaching, because though he made appointments and commitments, he failed to keep them. He didn't want to look at himself and instead kept asking me to "fix" his team. It was a frustrating coaching engagement that was doomed to failure.

Is *your* culture a safe and nurturing one? By focusing on this first C, a company leader can begin to move the company from a toxic working environment to one that is safe and nurturing.

TIP: Survey employees like a millennial would. Consider using any of these twenty-first century survey tools, making anonymous and valuable feedback easy to gather and assess. Search online for PropFuel, SurveyMonkey Engage, Workify, DecisionWise, TinyPulse, HR-Survey, and NBRI (bundled services). New tools come on the market all the time, so check frequently for the latest features.

DETERMINING YOUR CORE VALUES

Whether or not they are acknowledged and communicated, every organization has core values that form the basis for the company culture and govern what gets rewarded. It makes sense then that, before considering how core values might be changed to create a more positive and productive culture, managers need to understand the core values that are already in place.[23]

BEST PRACTICES: LIVING YOUR CORE VALUES

Core values are *personal*, and they reflect the personality of your company and how it is perceived by customers, vendors, and affiliates. Time and thought must be given to voicing the values of the company and its culture. Declaring, "We have integrity!" is simply not enough.

Importantly, company leaders must determine up front the values that they can live by and stand by. As Salesforce leaders and employees have pointed out on their own company website, the company must be willing to part with anyone who cannot live and work the company's core values—even if it means financial sacrifice. The understanding has to be that the corrosive damage to the company and all of its members would be much, much greater than any single incident or loss.

Area Floors, a Pacific Northwest flooring company, grappled with just such a decision—and then went public with results. After carefully rolling out the company's core values, CEO Brandy Marsh

---

23 Jim Collins, in his book *Good to Great (New York: Harper Business, 2001), offers a "Mission to Mars" exercise that provides a great opportunity to identify your company's core values.*

realized she had a test case on her hands: a long-term, top-performing sales rep who continually defied the company's core value of "Ownership mentality," which ensured that all employees would operate on the basis of long-term gain for the company, not short-term, self-interested benefit. The rep was warned once for blatantly flaunting the core values with improper behavior and inappropriate use of resources, but the behavior persisted and the sales rep was terminated, sending a message to all. (Junior sales reps stepped up and eventually became stars.) The overall employee reaction was "Thank you for promoting and being serious about a culture of integrity and values in an industry where it is rare! We love working at Area Floors!"[24]

This understanding of the danger posed by lax core values is essential in "topgrading," a corporate hiring and interviewing methodology originally conceived to identify preferred candidates for a particular position, but often used to evaluate current employees as well. Individuals are graded ABC via a four-quadrant chart with two axis lines: one axis indicates performance, the other indicates adherence to core values. An individual who scores high on the performance axis, yet violates the core values along the other axis, is considered a B/C performer. That employee can constitute a dangerous and disruptive force that could undermine the entire culture of the organization—even if that individual is a senior officer of the corporation.

---

24 Marcus Buckingham writes about the importance of understanding and playing to your strengths in his books *Now, Discover Your Strengths (Washington DC: Gallup Press, 2001)* and *Go Put Your Strengths to Work (New York: Free Press, 2007)*, both suggested reading for employees and their managers.

BEST PRACTICES: COMMUNICATING YOUR CORE VALUES

Core values are so much a part of a successful company's lifeblood that when I coached executives at Bristol-Myers Squibb, the company's core values were the screensavers on every computer screen in the organization. No employee could begin his or her day without being reminded just how essential the company's values were. Other companies conspicuously post their core values at their building entrances and up front on their websites so that not just their employees, but also customers and vendors, will know precisely "who" the company is, what it believes in, and how it will interact with the world. Some organizations have even developed icons for their core values, ubiquitous across company offices.

And last year, when I was coaching the head of human resources at AMAG Pharmaceuticals (a rapidly growing public pharmaceutical company based in Waltham, Massachusetts), I was delighted to discover that the company had literally translated its core values into "do's and don'ts" so that its workforce would suffer no confusion about how to live those values. The company was basically telling its employees, "Here's our core value, and here's what it means to live it or not to live it." The do's and don'ts even extended to hiring, promoting, and firing people, which made my HR client's expected work ethic within the company crystal clear.

Anyone who has shopped at Whole Foods will tell you that the innovative grocery retailer conspicuously posts photographic portraits of those employees who consistently demonstrate the company's eight well-communicated core values. Calling out exceptional employees is not just an internal exercise, either: at the company's bi-level stores, customers and suppliers cannot ride the escalators without viewing each and every recognized employee.

At Massachusetts-based Exclusive Concepts, a digital marketing agency where I coached company execs, a "postcard" approach was employed to communicate the company's core values. A large board had been placed at the workers' entrance/exit, with a supply of cards alongside. Workers were urged to fill out and pushpin a card onto the board every time they spied a coworker living the core values of the company. The board was routinely filled with cards that reported sightings such as "I saw Joe Smith run out to help a woman whose car was stuck outside our building. He lives our core value of *service to the community.*" Or, "Carol Cooper came in on Saturday morning to help after the steam leak. She said she wanted to help because she cared about what would happen to all the paperwork affected (not even her department) if it had to wait for Monday morning. Carol *cares.*"

TIP: Lay out your company's core values as relatable do's and don'ts. To prevent your company culture from being a disconnected one, consider grouping clear, concrete examples of positive and negative behaviors under core value headings such as: "Being collaborative," "Focusing on results," "Being transparent," and more.

Negative collaborative behaviors, for instance, are "Showing disrespect" or "Shutting down conversations you don't agree with." On the other hand, some positive collaborative behaviors are "Welcoming other points of view" and "Being open to constructive feedback."

MILLENNIALS AND THE CULTURE DIVIDE

I recently began working with a West Coast staffing firm headed up by a new, young CEO, Isabel. Isabel told me that the company was having difficulty attracting, retaining, and motivating their millennial workers to work as hard as employees had done in the past. The bad news: 80 percent of the company's workforce was under the age of thirty-five.

Isabel contacted me for executive coaching and I explained that I would work with her and her team using my powerful 7Cs approach, plus a proven methodology called "Scaling Up"[25] (to work on people, strategy, execution, and cash). One-on-one executive coaching with the company's new leader would also ensure the 7Cs would trickle down throughout the organization.

I began by working with the team on the first C of Culture. Together, we mapped out precisely how to build a strong foundation for the company through the creation of well-defined core values plus a clearly communicated mission and vision statement for the company. In my initial meeting with the team, I learned that despite twenty years of growth, they had never considered core values and thus had none. They also had no real vision regarding where the company was headed, let alone how it was going to get there.

We all began to work together to create the core values of the company, which led us to a discussion of the culture of the company in the age of millennials, and the challenges the company had been

---

25 Scaling Up and the book of the same name are award-winning follow-ons to Verne Harnish's 2002 bestseller *Mastering the Rockefeller Habits (Ashburn, VA: Gazelles, 2002). Both works form the core of Gazelles Inc. (of which I am a member). Gazelles* provides executive education, coaching, and technology services to business leaders and their companies around the world. Free business resources and growth tools helpful to 7Cs work are available from www.gazelles. com.

facing in recruiting and retaining talent (largely millennial hires) in a full-employment economy. As I complete the writing of this book, Isabel, her team, and I will be working through the rest of the 7Cs to ensure that the company is well on its way to inspiring—not just motivating—accountability.

It's no surprise that millennials (and a good number of their Gen X predecessors) gravitate toward companies in industries and professions where core values such as "fun," "work/life balance," and "caring" are not only communicated, but well-lived. Many companies are acutely aware of the millennials' need to work in environments with such core values, for most millennials have no experience working in a command-and-control workplace reminiscent of eras they've only heard about. This is a generation bred on social media, taught schoolwork via computer gaming, and accustomed to twenty-four seven, on-demand service (not just during waking or working hours).

For instance, millennials do not internally grasp the notion of "watching the clock" at work because they don't ordinarily use clocks or wear watches. Because many of them do not care about owning cars, they don't save up for them and often Uber or bike to work instead. The real estate industry is steeling itself for difficult times ahead because millennials also are not motivated to buy starter homes (which then erodes the secondary market for trading up to larger homes). Marriage and family plus auto and home ownership was the dream of generations that preceded millennials, but it is not necessarily *their* dream.

In short, millennials' core values are vastly different from the ones that drove many traditional industries and professions such as finance, investment banking, and law. The values that greased the wheels of these verticals—make partner, earn enough money to buy a big house in the suburbs—mean very little to millennials. They want to have fun at work, create something amazing, take risks to innovate (even if they have to keep starting over), change the world (for the better), and then play hard and hang with friends when they are not working—equally as important to them as work.

A company's twenty-first century core values may need to be quite different than they were in the twentieth century in order to serve the company well and, at the same time, inspire millennials to their fullest levels of accountability. Most significantly, a company's culture must provide safety in which employees can speak their minds and even

> ## MILLENNIALS' CORE VALUES ARE VASTLY DIFFERENT FROM THE ONES THAT DROVE MANY TRADITIONAL INDUSTRIES AND PROFESSIONS SUCH AS FINANCE, INVESTMENT BANKING, AND LAW.

question authority. Millennials, more than any other generation, will not contribute in an unsafe environment.

Raised by a generation of boomers whose goal as parents was to make their children feel safe in a chaotic world, millennials will remove themselves quickly from environments where they cannot speak up, share their views and ideas, and lobby for change and innovation. Remember: they seek mentorship and collaboration. Without your support to help them delight you with their contributions to your goals and those of the enterprise, they will go elsewhere or work on their own. These young workers are not afraid to strike out on their own as their parents and grandparents may have been, and they often have little in the way of material possessions or family responsibility to risk.

In the following chapters, we'll tackle the next six of the 7Cs—all of which are enabled by a safe, inspiring culture. Those Cs will help you quickly reduce disengagement and dramatically boost employee accountability across *all* of the generations in your workplace. Read on to find out how to stoke your company's engine for decades by inspiring, not demanding, accountability.

TAKING ACTION: WHERE IS YOUR COMPANY ON THE CULTURE CONTINUUM?

1. **Conduct a quick search online for "Best Companies to Work For"** and "Best Places for Millennials to Work" plus similar lists.

2. **Scan the lists for any organization that is either** (a) a direct competitor, (b) a company in another vertical with any similarities to your own, or (c) a company you admire in any vertical.

3. **Make a list of five of those companies and conduct a quick search** for each organization's core values. Check first for commonalities across the company values. Does *your* company communicate and reinforce those same values?

4. **Now check the companies' values for values that are conspicuously absent** from your own company values. Might those values make a difference to your company culture if

they were adopted, well communicated, and reinforced?

5. **Consider discussing your discoveries and conclusions with your leadership team** members, as a way to open an assessment of where your company lies on the culture continuum, and how new efforts to create a culture of safety for all employees might dramatically improve engagement and accountability for your organization.

CHAPTER FIVE

LET'S BE CLEAR

If you are not clear, nothing is going to happen.

—**Diane von Furstenberg, iconic American fashion designer**

In the previous chapter on creating a culture of safety, we discovered that a culture that thrives on inquiry and dialogue actively encourages contribution and innovation. One of the reasons for that should not be hard to understand: company employees need to feel safe to ask questions, so that they can get greater *clarity* about the job at hand. With clarity, anything is possible—including the highest levels of engagement, accountability, contribution, and innovation.[26]

THE C THAT MAKES ALL OTHER CS POSSIBLE

In the process of working on executive-level coaching with her own team, Carole, a vice president in a global communications firm, realized that (somewhat ironically for a communications pro) she needed to refresh her own skills communicating with her people.

---

26 Business guru Patrick Lencioni has written extensively on the importance of clarity. His book *The Advantage: Why Organizational Health Trumps Everything Else In Business (San Francisco: Jossey-Bass, 2012)* is suggested reading.

Confusion had surfaced regarding the tasks required to ensure the division's new two-year strategy. Balls had been dropped, blame had been liberally applied, team members seemed disgruntled, and some of the newer and younger employees had abandoned ship. Worse, the ability to move forward was not improving as it should.

"I don't understand why people aren't 'getting it,'" Carole complained. "We've had meeting after meeting, and I've made it plain that they're all missing their goals and falling short, performance-wise. I've been crystal clear about what I want, and I've lit a fire under them, yet they're still not delivering! How can I get them to do what I need them to do?"

Carole's complaints aren't unusual ones, and her approach—holding *more* meetings wherein she cracks the whip even harder—is common. But if she had been a fly on the wall, she might have heard eye-opening gripes as her people left the room: "I wasn't even trained for that!" or "How does she think *that's* going to happen with not enough staff? I have too much on my desk already!"

To get the message of *reciprocal* clarity across to her, I asked Carole, "Can you recall a time in your own career when you couldn't get the clarity that *you* needed from a manager?"

She frowned for a moment and then looked as though she was experiencing an "aha" recollection. "When I was just starting out," she confided, "I had a job where the woman training me would throw a hundred details at me each day, and there was just no time to take notes about every single process. After a few days, I went back to her to get clarification on one of the things she had told me, and she said, 'I'm not going to repeat it. I said it once and if you didn't get it, you'll just have to figure it out. I don't have time to babysit you.' Of course I was petrified to go back and ask her anything else, so I searched for someone who could help me out, but no one else knew how to do anything well, either. They were all too scared to ask for more information. I never forgot that experience."

Then I asked Carole to think about her own employees—especially her newer millennial workers, particularly vulnerable to feeling insecure in the workplace. I asked if she had made the following clear, so that the tasks could be satisfactorily completed by her team.

- Had she handed down tasks that were formed through the use of **SMART** goals?

- That is, had the assignments been **Specific?** (Or were they somewhat vague?)

- Were the results **Measurable?** (Would her people know when they had achieved the goal?)

- Were they **Attainable?** (Would her team members or others have control over the goals? Would goals be attainable at their skill levels, and with their workloads, for instance?)

- Were the goals **Relevant** to her people? (Or were they alien to their work culture or to their ethical backgrounds, for instance?)

- And were the goals **Time-bound?** (What was the deadline for each part of the work, and the work as a whole? Were the deadlines possible to achieve, or unrealistic and designed only to impress clients and senior management and "spur" the team on?)

- Was Carole helping her team members succeed in their initiatives by making it safe to achieve **Clarity** in all the other 7C areas?

- Was clarity in all things a basis of the team **Culture** that Carole had created for herself and her people? Was clarity an essential component of the company culture? Would the nurturing of clarity in her group's culture help to improve her company's culture? (Answer to this last question: of course!)

- Was it safe for the team members to bring up and get clarity on issues of **Capacity?** ("Right now, I don't have sufficient time or resources to do what you've asked me to do by the deadline requested.")

- Was it safe for team members to bring up issues of **Competence** or **Confidence** so that roles could be clarified? ("I'm concerned that I won't be able to deliver this as quickly as you need." Or, "I do not have the skills or skill level to manage this task without more training. Can this task be swapped with or handed off to someone else?)

- Was it safe for team members to apprise her of personal issues and thus be clear about things that might impact **Capacity** and **Commitment** to do the job at hand? ("I can't work the weekends that would be needed to get this done in time, because of family issues.") Or was it plain that their manager did not care?

- Was it safe for team members to confidentially bring up issues regarding their **Compensation?** (I'm not getting paid adequately to do this, or to work overtime.) Did Carole understand how not addressing and clarifying compensation issues might affect outcomes?

ATTAINING CLARITY: THE ROLE OF THE MANAGER

To put it simply, *the role of the manager is to hold him or herself accountable for the hearing of the listener.* That means it is *your* job, as your employees' manager, to make sure your teams are completely clear about what you are asking them to do. (Remember our second tip box? It was to create a screensaver or desk placard that always reminds you: "*My* Job Is to Help You Do *Your* Job.")

> THAT MEANS IT IS *YOUR* JOB, AS YOUR EMPLOYEES' MANAGER, TO MAKE SURE YOUR TEAMS ARE COMPLETELY CLEAR ABOUT WHAT YOU ARE ASKING THEM TO DO.

The truth is, it has to be okay for your team members to ask: How good is good enough? How fast is fast enough? How much is enough? Without that clarity (as Ms. von Furstenberg, the source of our opening quotation has pointed out) nothing is going to happen. At least, nothing good. The amazing thing is, even if you don't believe you have the time to think through every single step of an assignment before you present it to your group, you can achieve clarity with one safe and simple tool perfectly designed to invite the inquiry you need. Just ask: "Do you have any questions?"

And mean it.

DON'T STEP ON LANGUAGE OR COMMUNICATION STYLE

Then, pay attention to your language during the ensuing dialogues, for there is nuance in language. You don't want to unwittingly undermine your good work in eliciting inquiry by quashing your employees' initiative with language that does not mirror their own.

For instance, if a team member feels safe enough to bring up "We're slammed with orders this week and are struggling to get them out the door before we can take on anything else," you wouldn't want to respond with "I guess you're a little backed up. Maybe I can give you an extra day." A more caring and validating response would be to mirror the original language and thus open the door for inquiry: "I'm so sorry you are slammed this week. When do you anticipate you'll be ready to take on the new initiative, and how can I help you get to it as quickly as possible?"

As for communication style, remember our earlier story in Chapter One about the two publishing executives, Lydia and Walter, who could not communicate with each other? She was hired to launch a new publishing imprint and was chatty, virtually bursting with new ideas; he was old-school and preferred communication distilled to its essence. Does your team include such disparate personality types? To fine-tune your communication with team members and get a better handle on how your communication styles mesh, consider personality assessment tools such as DISC, Myers-Briggs (MBTI), Predictive Index, Hogan Assessments, or EQ-I (for emotional intelligence assessment). All are perusable in quick Google searches, and many may be ideal to introduce at team and management retreats or during the hiring process.

IT'S NOT WEAKNESS, IT'S INFO SHARING

I've had plenty of coaching clients who walked in my door misguidedly proud of their "no excuses" approach to management. But I've also known strong leaders who champion an edict that actually *works*: "No surprises!"

As I've pointed out, the reason "no surprises" is such a powerful statement is that while "no excuses" informs workers you are not interested in hearing anything they have to say about completing their tasks and meeting their goals, "no surprises" inspires just the opposite: it encourages and supports *two-way* clarity. Yes, "no surprises" tells your people what is important to *you*, but it also urges *your people* to tell you anything and everything they can, at any time, to prevent initiatives from going off the rails.

"No surprises" says: "Share whatever information you've got, no matter how scary it might be to share it. It is safe to tell me anything that will impact the work, and I want and need that information. The important thing is that we are all pulling together for the good of the company, and if the company succeeds, we all succeed."

Even workers from ethnic and national cultures where the admission of failure can imply weakness come to appreciate the "no surprises" principle when it is reinforced throughout the entire corporate culture. Companies like Google and Southwest Airlines—both populated by a demographic of vastly different country cultures, religions, and creeds—have consistently ranked as Best Places to Work because they treat their employees as company *owners* who are relied on to speak up about anything and everything that might keep the company from success.

BEST PRACTICES: Create a clear "fishbowl" culture. One company manager came up with the "fishbowl" concept of fostering clarity because she believed that "When employees have the full context about a decision and the options considered, they are more likely to support it."[27] The "fishbowl" meetings were designed to flesh out new proposals and, even within time constraints, give everyone a chance to be educated about key decisions.

Here's how they work: One ring of employees sits in an inner circle, exchanging ideas and committing to nonpartisan inquiry, to learn all they can about the subjects at hand. At the same time, another ring of employees forms a larger outer circle "gallery," to benefit from the wholly transparent inquiry process and exchange of ideas. Because only one ring actively participates as the other ring benefits, the process moves swiftly and can be instituted frequently.

THE MANAGER AS COACH

Turning the manager into a coach may not be a new concept, but have you ever stopped to think how advantageous it would be to acquire some of the essential skills of coaching? That's because, first and foremost, an effective coach is a good *listener*. And a manager cannot effect any real change in productivity without receiving highly valuable information from employees by listening to what they have to say. Steven Covey said it best when he quoted the Bible for his

---

27   Marcus Erb, "How to Inspire an Ownership Spirit Among Employees," *Entrepreneur*, March 15, 2011, https://www.entrepreneur.com/article/219328.

book *The 7 Habits of Highly Effective People*: "Seek first to understand, then to be understood."

Yet, managers frequently cringe at the idea of coaching—even in the new age of millennials who not only welcome coaching from their managers, but seek it. Ironically, though, it is coaching that could be a manager's most direct and mutually beneficial route to connecting with millennials.[28] Interestingly, though the press on millennial attributes is now widespread, and companies everywhere are struggling to attract and retain this generation of workers, managers continue to insist they have little time for mentoring these employees or acting as a counselor to them.

IT IS COACHING THAT COULD BE A MANAGER'S MOST DIRECT AND MUTUALLY BENEFICIAL ROUTE TO CONNECTING WITH MILLENNIALS.

But wait. Don't confuse the terms coach, mentor, and counselor. A *mentor* is responsible for teaching and modeling behavior for his or her charges—always beneficial, but not always possible, time-wise, for managers (savvy managers find other ways to set up mentoring programs for their people, however). Being a *counselor* presumes the ability to give expert advice to another individual (also beneficial if one can get expert advice for free, but not a requirement of a coach's skill set, either).

The fact is, the most important skill of a coach is *asking powerful questions* to deepen the thinking of the individual being coached,

---

28 Eighty-three percent of millennials who have a workplace coach or mentor are satisfied with this aspect of their working lives, according to the 2016 Deloitte Millennial Survey, https://www2.deloitte.com/content/dam/Deloitte/global/Documents/About-Deloitte/gx-millenial-survey-2016-exec-summary.pdf.

and then *suggesting or eliciting action steps* that will be effective for all involved: employee, manager, and team members. Here's an example:

Manager/coach: What might help you get to the finish line on the Johnson project? Please think about roles, added assistance, whatever you feel will be most effective most quickly.

Team member: Hmmm, let me think … If you could pull John off the division's budget-planning exercise this week and let me have him on the finance side of this project, that would help immensely. Then, if we could train another team member to handle finance issues on these types of projects in the future, we'd never be caught short.

Manager/coach: Both excellent solutions. I'll move John over today. In the meantime, if you'll query the team members about who wants to train for the new finance spot on these projects, and then locate a cost-effective training solution, I'll sign off on the training dollars immediately.

TIP: Clarity starts at home. If you don't enable dialogue at work, you probably don't have it at home, either. When it comes to the big C of Clarity (which, again, impacts all the other Cs):

- Are you constantly having arguments at home with your spouse and/or your kids because they don't understand what you expect of them?

- Do they tell you that they feel like they're always disappointing you?

- Do you resort to punishment tactics because they don't do what you expect of them?

If so, look to your own behavior and your ability to establish clarity around your expectations through honest inquiry and safe dialogue. Make it safe for family members to ask questions, give feedback, and disagree with you. Then, practice your inquiry and listening skills to help achieve better clarity for all.

THE MANAGER AS PRIORITIZER

We'll be talking about prioritization in detail in the following chapter, but first and foremost, prioritization is essential to clarity. In fact, when clarity breaks down, it usually breaks down at the juncture of prioritization. As more and more tasks and projects are added to the team to-do list, with little to identify which item is more important than the next (and why), the team's very goals and mission become obscured. There are simply too many things listed as priorities or key initiatives. In a rapidly changing business environment where *everything* seems urgent, managers who strive to achieve clarity for their teams learn how to prioritize for their people quickly, effectively, even on the fly. In his book *Getting Things Done: The Art of Stress-Free Productivity*,[29] David Allen emphasizes that time management is all about priority management.

---

29   David Allen, *Getting Things Done: The Art of Stress-Free Productivity (New York: Viking, 2001).*

CLARIFYING ROLES

In rapidly changing work environments, roles are constantly shifting, employees are being asked to do more things that they've never done before, and individuals are hired to tackle jobs that haven't existed previously. In workplaces where achieving role clarity is tantamount to describing a moving target, it is vital that people are encouraged to ask questions, seek feedback, make mistakes, and even fail and try again as they don't just live their new roles, but help to create them.

In a work environment where new roles spring up daily, helping to clarify and define roles becomes the job of worker and manager alike. Workplace cultures that not only are safe for ongoing inquiry and dialogue, but encourage risk taking to develop new roles, are those that are most agile, innovative, and future looking. (No coincidence that they are also meccas for millennial workers.) Silicon Valley workforces, for instance, are comfortable with a certain level of ambiguity, but that doesn't mean it is not a manager's responsibility to help workers define, fulfill, and expand their roles via the encouragement of ongoing two-way dialogue. (Gazelles offers a free and powerful exercise called the FACe, or Function Accountability Chart, which helps a team define who is responsible for what and how each individual's performance will be measured with leading and lagging indicators.)

CLARIFYING DECISION RIGHTS AND DEADLINES

How often do managers hand off tasks without ensuring that the authority (decision rights) to achieve those tasks are clearly stated? Answer: way too often. In fact, fuzzy ownership of decision rights is a leading cause of bottlenecked productivity, as is not providing a clear picture of decision-making *limits*. Then too, there is often more than one individual accountable for a role, with little clarity about who the final point person is.

TIP: It takes a tree. Having trouble clarifying decision rights? Try this widely used tree model.[30]

The *leaves* of a tree can drop without damage to the company tree, so a staffer can be 100 percent responsible for those decisions; no need to inform the manager. (At the Ritz-Carlton Hotel Company, for instance, customer service reps can spend up to $1,000 on the spot, to "leaf-solve" a customer relations problem.)

If a *branch* breaks off, the tree can still survive, so the team member can make the decision, act on it, and report it within normal reporting frequency, to be tracked.

For more vulnerable *trunk* decisions, the staffer can make the decision but will need supervisor approval before enactment.

Root decisions can kill the company tree, so a team member must surface the issue for joint (leadership team) discussion and decision.

---

30 Susan Scott, *Fierce Conversations: Achieving Success at Work and In Life One Conversation at a Time* (New York: Penguin Putnam, 2004).

SMART MANAGERS, DECISION TREES, AND DIALOGUE

After a recent two-day workshop I conducted for a small high-tech company, the CEO phoned me to tell me she was reorganizing the company.

"It's now clear I'm doing too many things myself, and so I'm promoting one of my people to be in charge of all operations. We're in the process of creating clarity around decision-making authority." The tree diagram described in the previous tip was helping her push decision making down as far as possible.

"I want people to come to me with a solution recommendation after having thought through the problem," she said. "I don't want them asking me what to do unless it's a root problem!"

The same need for clarity goes for deadlines, too. For without that clarity, every project either is urgent or drops to the bottom of the pile along with everything else carrying no real deadline. But a smart manager is, first, a SMART manager: one who achieves clarity through SMART goals. Yet, what if the speed of modern-day business makes that kind of diligence less than possible? A responsible manager relies on an ability to keep the two-way dialogue open and driven by inquiry: "Do you have questions? Are you clear about the decision-making authority here? How about the deadlines?"

THE DAILY HUDDLE: CLARIFYING BOTTLENECKS

Many companies now employ what's called a daily "huddle" wherein team levels (smaller groups within a team) meet daily for very brief time periods strictly to identify bottlenecks and thus enable the team to move forward quickly and effectively. In eight to twelve minutes, priorities are shared, problems are uncovered, and team cohesion is reinforced.[31] The purpose of the meeting is not to solve the problems at the meeting, but to quickly apprise all of work status and keep everyone connected to the team's goals.

The point here is that the huddle is an exercise in sharing and listening. Whether the manager is present at huddles or relies on a team member to relay bottleneck information, the huddle also is an ideal opportunity for the manager, as coach, to quickly grasp issues that can be followed up later on with more in-depth meetings for troubleshooting. Global organizations or those with remote workers now make use of videoconferencing or social technologies to enable their huddles. Go online to check out platforms such as Slack, WhatsApp, Flock, Troop Messenger, HipChat, Chatwork, Microsoft Teams, Facebook Messenger, and more.

Whatever you do, though, don't confuse the need for huddle meetings with periodic "all hands" meetings wherein company leadership clearly communicates company vision, mission, and the current path to both. And don't forget: two-way communication between team members and managers should be an *ongoing* process to achieve clarity; it does not wait for periodic meetings or rely solely on huddles. Remember: no clarity, no accountability.

---

31   See Verne Harnish, *Scaling Up* (Ashburn, VA: Gazelles, 2014).

TAKING ACTION: LISTENING SELF-ASSESSMENT FOR MANAGERS

When it comes to your listening skills, ask yourself the following questions to reveal your current ability to achieve clarity:

1. **Do I ordinarily welcome and value information my team members impart to me?** Or do I usually know how I want to proceed?

2. **How well am I able to quiet myself to listen to and take in important information?** Or do I routinely multitask when others converse with me?

3. **How well do I comprehend and make it my goal to understand what is being presented to me?** Or do I routinely offer knee-jerk reactions without giving the conversation careful thought?

4. **Do I listen nonjudgmentally, or do I routinely filter conversations or dismiss information** by catching only phrases and words such as "can't do," "no time," "compensation," and "family issues"?

5. **Am I guilty of the common manager's habit of "half-listening"?**

6. **When was the last time I moved away from my desk, turned off my cell phone,** closed my door, and pulled up a chair opposite a team

member to hear what he or she had to say, with no distractions and without interrupting?

7. **Do I know the difference between asking questions that will help others to deeply consider issues, and interrogation?**

8. **I don't want to be a mentor or counselor. Do I appreciate the differences between coaching, mentoring, and counseling my employees?**

9. **How would I feel about my staff members being interviewed or surveyed** about my ability to welcome or elicit their questions and truly listen to them?

10. **If my team indicates that I need better inquiry and listening skills, would I be willing to work on those skills?**

CHAPTER SIX

CAPACITY: THE C WE DON'T SEE

Not knowing what else to do, the man began unloading the packs from the donkey's back and placed the entire load on the mule. Then, leaving the donkey where he had fallen, the man and the mule continued the journey. The mule, groaning beneath his heavy burden, said to himself, If I had only been willing to help the poor donkey, I would now be bearing half the load I carry—and would have a friend besides.

—Jeremiah 7:5

More than any other C, Capacity is the one that managers have the hardest time seeing, for four main reasons:

1. Managers often have so much work on their own desks, they feel they have little or no time to assess the workload of others.

2. Many managers don't *want* to know that their employees have too much work. (Some, unfortunately, prefer to suspect that their employees don't have enough work.)

3. Managers simply don't ask their employees about their workload before assigning new work.

4. Many workers don't feel safe saying to their boss that they are overloaded and can't accomplish the task requested of them in the time desired.

Jordan worked as the communications director for an independent school in the Northeast that, with the institution of a new head of school, was undergoing massive change and rapid growth. Jordan liked to call himself a "communications machine," but even he was beginning to buckle under the strain of working for an overly ambitious administrator who was determined to move the institution to new heights in record time.

Jordan's job had expanded in all directions, and each day brought numerous lengthy meetings, stacks of new project files, and hundreds of emails as his boss shot off missives to Jordan each time a new thought, idea, or task occurred to him. The emails arrived day and night, from dinnertime to dawn and every weekend. Jordan struggled to prioritize the workload but had difficulty discerning which assignments were urgent and which were "Hey, I was just thinking …" emails.

The damn finally broke one Friday afternoon when Jordan's boss spied him on his email at 5:00 p.m. "What are you reading emails for when I've been waiting for the notes on the new master plan?" he wanted to know.

Jordan responded that he had no way of knowing about the master plan notes, because the email about it was probably buried in the hundreds of assignments and messages his boss had sent him over the past few days. He was so inundated, he said, that he couldn't do anything until he read, sorted, and prioritized the mail.

"Those messages can't be just from *me*," said the headmaster, so Jordan showed him. "I had no idea …" was all his boss could utter.

This story is particularly memorable to me because Jordan's boss had absolutely no sense of his top staffer's capacity overload—and yet *he* was the one directly responsible for it.

Not long after, Jordan and some of his colleagues got together and compared notes. To a person, everyone felt completely overwhelmed by the new school leader. A few were considering leaving. Then, one of the staffers contacted a friend who served on the school's board of directors. She apprised the board member that everyone at the school had undergone a rigorous review process—everyone except the new head of school.

Shortly thereafter, a confidential staff-wide review of the top executive was instituted. Soon after that, the board members decreed that the new school leader could send out no more emails after 4:00 p.m. on school days, and none on weekends. They also insisted the new head undergo executive coaching. I was then brought in to help an overeager headmaster better understand what havoc his self-inflicted capacity issues were wreaking with nearly all of his reports and *their* reports.

The results were startling. Staffers were surveyed about their workloads. Goals and priorities were reassessed, and many were simply dropped. The headmaster's mission and vision were realigned with that of the institution. Timelines and workgroups were reconfigured. The head was directed to get out of his office each day and sit in on classes, sports activities, and study groups. Instead of going to lunch with the board, he enjoyed lunch with his teachers and reports. Most of all, he asked questions of his staffers and *listened*.

Two months later, my coaching client admitted, "Thank heavens I had no choice but to accept the board's decree and get some insight! I never realized that taking on way too much was not only overwhelming everyone on my staff, but it was actually preventing us from focusing on the goals that are aligned with our school's mission and our vision for the next five years. We were all so buried in email and daily tasks, nothing I really wanted to accomplish was actually getting done!"

The fact is, smaller businesses across all industries and professions struggle with capacity issues more than large businesses do, simply because in larger organizations there are greater numbers of people, each with more narrowly defined roles, as opposed to fewer workers each wearing multiple hats in smaller organizations. Yet the job of *all* company leaders and managers is to manage process (the "how" of work), priorities (aligning work goals with company mission and vision), and people (your most valuable resource and the lifeblood of your company). Capacity cuts across all three of your management commitments to your company.

YES IS A DIRTY WORD

Larger well-run companies often understand it's their business to know how long specific tasks take to accomplish. Many professions such as law, accounting, and consulting cannot even bill their clients without measuring the time to complete tasks. But it's rare for an employee in a smaller company to assess and clearly communicate just how long it will take to clear up everything on his or her plate. Thus, when a boss tells an employee, "I need you to do something," the employee reflexively replies, "Yes," while the manager assumes capacity is infinitely stretchable. The equation then becomes: the more a worker is asked to do, the more will get done. (And we haven't even touched on the stigma attached to telling a boss, "I can't" or "I won't.")

Unfortunately, too many employees are left to juggle priorities on their own and figure out how they will get their work done, all the while feeling there is far too much on their plate. They wind up pulled in endless directions. Baby boomers have grudgingly suffered through such capacity issues for decades, which may explain why they currently demonstrate the highest disengagement figures of all the working generations.[32] Gen Xers are not as passive-aggressive as boomers; they may or may not stick, depending on the market. Millennials, on the other hand, are averse to capacity creep and have no problem making for the door when the work environment overwhelms them.[33]

> ## TOO MANY EMPLOYEES ARE LEFT TO JUGGLE PRIORITIES ON THEIR OWN AND FIGURE OUT HOW THEY WILL GET THEIR WORK DONE

Right now, the prospect of millennial flight may not concern some company heads. One of my clients, the CEO of a $100 million multidivisional sales firm, has been attracting "sales stars" with a high-incentive compensation system that rewards "smart, hungry, driven employees" for the volume of clients they bring on board.

---

32 "There's a Generation Gap in Your Workplace," Gallup, August 6, 2013, https://news.gallup.com/businessjournal/163466/generation-gap-workplace.aspx.

33 According to a 2018 study commissioned by the digital and cloud communications company Jive, the average millennial has already had three jobs, and most millennials look for another job before they hit the three-year mark. Nearly a quarter of millennials are at a job for only six months to a year before they start looking elsewhere. Another 30 percent start hunting after twelve months. (Karissa Neely, "New Study Commissioned by Utah Business Looks at What Millennials Really Want at Work," *Daily Herald*, January 14, 2018, https://www.heraldextra.com/business/local/new-study-commissioned-by-utah-business-looks-at-what-millennials/article_39e47aa7-11c8-54a2-9917-08d27f3dffcc.html.)

Many of the company's sales stars put in eighty-hour weeks and earn solid six-figure incomes before they are twenty-five. When they burn out and leave, the company looks for others to take their place.

Yet, in the new age of millennials, turnover has been a good deal more rapid than anyone anticipated. I recently asked the CEO of this sales firm, "How will you run a twenty-first century organization poised to succeed in the decades ahead, with a constantly rotating workforce?" I pointed out that for most enterprises, the cost of hiring, onboarding, training, and then losing valuable workers[34] is high, while the payback for a loyal, engaged, results-oriented workforce is much greater.

This newly enlightened CEO is coming to understand that "Yes" is not what a smart manager should want to hear from an overloaded worker. "Yes" doesn't tell you that your staffers love their work, are inspired to be accountable for top-flight results, and want to persevere to help take your team and your company to its next levels. In short, an effective manager does not want Capacity to be the C not seen.

We have more work to do, and a few more Cs to grapple with, but this client is determined to move his firm into the coming decade poised for greater and greater success. He is now willing to lay groundwork today that will pay off big time tomorrow. Developing a plan to better manage capacity will help to curtail the spin of his revolving door, and ensure that his new millennial workforce remains engaged and results driven (accountable) for as long as possible.

---

34   Capacity overload is the first of "nine worst things that managers do that send good people packing," according to Travis Bradberry, "9 Things That Make Good Employees Quit, *The Huffington Post,* last modified December 6, 2017, https://www.huffingtonpost.com/dr-travis-bradberry/9-things-that-make-good-e_b_8870074.html.

THE MANY WAYS TO SEE (OR "C") CAPACITY ISSUES

CULTURE

A corporate culture wherein employees are safe (better yet, encouraged) to speak up about anything that may pose a process bottleneck or a threat to the company's mission or vision, undergirds all Cs and shapes an environment of accountability. In safe company cultures, employees feel free to let their bosses know when capacity issues may endanger the timely completion of tasks. In those safe cultures, managers make excellent use of the ongoing reciprocal conversation with their workers, to inquire at the assignment of a task or project, "Is there room to take on this project, or do we need to move some work to others and/or re-prioritize? I want to make sure you have the bandwidth to give this your full attention, so how can I help make that possible?"

IN SAFE COMPANY CULTURES, EMPLOYEES FEEL FREE TO LET THEIR BOSSES KNOW WHEN CAPACITY ISSUES MAY ENDANGER THE TIMELY COMPLETION OF TASKS.

A culture of daily huddles is the fail-safe to prevent bottlenecks due to capacity overload. In a small group of team members, it's easy to quickly inform a manager and teammates, "I'm concerned about getting this new initiative off the ground. I'll be traveling this week, and we only have one other team member who can get to this at once. Everyone else is working on the new booth and the keynote at the industry show. But this project requires at least two owners, maybe more. Let's meet later today to figure this out."

TIP: Steal my "Iceberg" graphic to anticipate problems. One of the simplest ways to get your team members thinking about problems that may be lurking under the surface—and may suddenly overload capacity, for instance—is to draw an image of an iceberg on a whiteboard or similar, for all team members to see.

One-quarter of the berg rises above sea level, while three-quarters hides below, deeper and much wider than the neat little peak that is visible.

Ask your people to scrawl next to the tip of the iceberg the issues readily apparent to all. Then ask them to start jotting down next to the massive berg beneath the things that no one has really been looking at—those issues, below the surface, that could overwhelm capacity and potentially sink your group or even company ship. You'll be amazed at how much latent information will suddenly surface. Clients tell me that this little exercise has yielded remarkable results, allowing an entire team to anticipate staffing shortages, training needs, recasting of job posts, and more.

Let us never forget the most important aspect of a culture of safety: when capacity overload looms, employees feel safe to come forward with that information. They also feel their commitment to care about their manager and their company. They appreciate their duty to alert you to issues that could become problems, bottlenecks, or catastrophes. "I'm way beyond capacity" is not a gripe or an indication of weakness or incompetence. It's a warning light that indicates that some quick intervention or troubleshooting is required to keep things humming along.

CLARITY

Of course, even in a safe culture—and one that employs daily huddles—progress can be stopped dead in its tracks by an obtuse manager who checks on capacity with "You'll make this happen, right?"

Clarity would enable that manager to prevent disasters such as nondelivery of results, delayed results, disappointing results, and/ or discouraged, disengaged, and nonaccountable workers ("It's not my fault we couldn't close that deal; what did he expect when we're already beyond capacity with three other deals ahead of it?").

But a simple "Tell me how you're doing with the tasks on your plate; do you have the capacity to take on another task right now?" is an inquiry that opens clarifying dialogue. The team member can respond with information regarding the status of the existing projects plus a quick assessment of room for new work. A smart manager in a safe culture would *not* want to hear "Sure." He or she would move the dialogue forward with additional inquiry that would help set up a *social contract* of sorts, which would ensure that the work will get done properly: "What stages are you in with your other initiatives and priorities? Let's quickly assess in case I need to find you more resources or move some responsibilities around. I need to make sure this will get done by our deadline."

Clarity serves not just to protect the employee from an unmanageable workload, but also an *employer* from capacity fiascos. Speaking recently with one of my client companies, I realized that the inability to clarify capacity expectations had caused serious problems. The

CEO of the growing US/Asia firm told me that she had a new leadership team hire who did not work out of the company's US headquarters in the Northeast but operated remotely from the Midwest, where he could also attend to a previous client on occasion. She confided that he was not managing the type of workload she had anticipated and that because they were in different locations, she felt his work was "invisible" to her. Mostly, she had expected him to be on the ground in Asia more often than he was. Now she felt he wasn't carrying his weight. She suspected she was paying full-time wages for half the work she had anticipated from him.

Regrettably, she had never really spelled out the volume and scope of work she expected from him and had never queried him for *specifics* about his bandwidth and priorities. She had told him that she needed him to "spend time overseas" but had never detailed how frequently he needed to travel, to do what, by which deadlines, and so on. Our work together helped her to confront these errors directly and reassess her recent hire's true capacity so that she could then decide whether to renegotiate terms, realign capacity vs. need, or replace him.

MORE CS TO HELP YOU MANAGE CAPACITY ISSUES

Even with additional inquiry and dialogue to obtain clarity on whether or not an employee's capacity levels can handle additional work, it is still up to the manager to determine if the Cs of Competence and Confidence are sufficient to handle the increased workload. Is the employee experienced enough and well trained to handle the type and velocity of assignments coming down the pike?

Then, too, the Compensation C may need to be adjusted for the additional work. And—even if the employee professes, "I love my job and don't mind working all the extra hours"—unrestricted expectations could exhaust the worker. That would also impair the company's C of Commitment to care about the welfare of its employees and not burn them out. (More about these additional Cs in the following chapters.)

CAPACITY, MILLENNIALS, AND WORK/LIFE BALANCE

Most millennials will tell you that few things are as important to them as work/life balance. Yet, in a traditional command-and-control work environment where employees are thought to deliver more the more they are "stretched," the first thing that must be sacrificed is the balance between an employee's productive work life and his or her recharging station: home, family, and personal interests.

Interestingly, many company leaders and their managers are only beginning to understand that faced with giving up those things in their lives that ensure happiness, health, and well-being, few millennials would remain in any conventional workplace. That is why so many workplaces are changing and are offering more "life" perks (day care, cleaners, gyms, etc.) on the work campus, enabling remote and virtual working, and urging workers to take their well-earned PTO days to refresh and recharge at home and in the outside world.

Millennials most certainly won't sacrifice their outside life interests because you've decided to ignore capacity issues and "stretch" them to deliver whatever you can squeeze out of them.

GET UP TO SPEED ON CAPACITY: YOUR TWELVE-STEP PROGRAM

Dealing with capacity issues that thwart employee productivity confounds many company leaders and managers. But it doesn't have to. As a professional coach and consultant, I routinely make use of an arsenal of effective tools to help my top-level management clients assess their team members' capacity, goals, potential for bottlenecks, and so on. Short of seeking expert help, here's a quick way you can reduce your group's delays in task and project completion while improving the disappointing project results you may have been experiencing.

1. **Get a snapshot of your team members' existing and ongoing capacity issues** by finding out via simple surveys: How long did it take them to do each of their most recent core tasks or project assignments? How long is their *actual* workday and workweek? (Ask them to track their work hours—including business email, call, and text time outside the office—for a week or two before they turn in their responses.) Ask them: What else is competing for your time? (Be prepared to hear "Too many meetings!")

2. **Look for patterns of delayed or disappointing project results** by going over the past few months' worth of group project results. How many projects were delayed? Plagued by issues? Not satisfactorily concluded?

3. **Ask your reports about their available capacity before you assign more work.** What does their current workload look like? How many days or hours will it take to complete

their current tasks? What are their *realistic* time estimates to complete new assignments, given the current workload?

4. **Review your reports' priority lists as soon as you can, and each time you assign new work.** How do they prioritize their current assignments? Is their assessment of priorities aligned with your own? How will they re-prioritize the current workload to accommodate your new assignment(s)? Help them to re-prioritize what is on their plates each time you add a task or project to that load. (Example: "Let's put the Burns project on hold for this week while you work on the agenda and speakers for the upcoming executive meeting in Atlanta. I can reassign the Smith project to Ben; he's got more availability this week than you do. Does this work for you?")

5. **Be specific about new project details and ask for specific recommendations** regarding extra time, resources, and timeline adjustments that may be needed to accomplish new tasks. Don't say, "If you have problems, handle them, but get this done." Rather, as you move through the description of the project and its full details, ask, for example: "Will you be able to get this amount of work done in the time I have estimated, or do we need to adjust the timeline to make this happen? Do you have *enough* resources and the *right* resources for this part of the project?"

6. **Check in frequently with team members, to assess status and catch bottlenecks before they happen.** Use daily/weekly quick huddles for status/bottleneck checks; follow-up meetings for joint troubleshooting.

7. **To free up capacity, make use of tech-enabled meeting and discussion platforms and other social media designed for business use.** Tools such as Yammer, Chanty, Slack, Salesforce Chatter, Jive, and Facebook Workplace can help workers get quick answers and feedback from coworkers and managers; they can also dramatically reduce daily and weekly hours spent in group meetings.

8. **To avoid creating unnecessary work that will ratchet up work volume,** resist the urge to "get people started" on projects that have not yet jelled. Also resist the impulse to hand off projects your own managers have initiated but not yet confirmed.

9. **Don't be a chronic mind changer or micromanager.** Lack of confidence in your own project design ability (or lack of trust in employees' ability to execute) may be a driver of capacity issues among your staffers. Seek coaching or training to help you confidently create project plans that can be assigned without constantly readjusting or rescinding them.

10. **No surprises! Make it safe for your reports not only to speak up about capacity issues when asked, but to proactively seek you out or speak up at meetings.** This is the absolute best way to make sure that you are always apprised of impending capacity bottlenecks that could devolve into serious problems. Empower your people to be lookouts for icebergs anywhere and everywhere they might surface.

11. **Be willing and able to step in and offer assistance to remediate bottlenecks.** It is up to you, the manager, to

quickly open up the standpipes of additional staff, needed support, and increased resources, or to help renegotiate deadlines and other constraints that may become barriers to satisfactory results. Remember, it is a manager's job to *help* employees do their jobs. If you cannot be accountable for your *own* commitment to the company, there is an excellent chance your reports will not be able to be accountable to *you*.

12. **Help to create a company culture that cares about the welfare and work/life balance of its workforce by making it safe for employees to speak up about capacity issues that overwhelm and disengage them.** Is your company culture tuned in to capacity overload? Watch for signs of disengagement and low morale, such as increased turnover or employees showing up late and missing days. Also keep an ear to team members' reports of growing complaints about workload levels from *their* reports. Importantly, do not dismiss as "employee capacity failure" family and life events such as illness, planned family vacations, and family emergencies. Rather, step in to troubleshoot capacity impact that may result from both natural and unexpected life occurrences. If you want your employees to return to work engaged and eager to contribute, recognize their right to planned-for or unanticipated downtime.

TAKE ACTION: CAPACITY SELF-ASSESSMENT FOR MANAGERS

The quiz below is designed primarily for senior leadership, directors, and other senior-level managers.

It is also applicable for mid-level managers over the general employee population.

Circle one of the four potential responses that follow each question. Then assess the areas that did not garner YES responses; these are areas that require attention and development. (I also advise clients to run through the assessment six months hence, to note areas of dramatic improvement and areas that still require attention.)

1. Do you know how long it takes your reports to complete their most frequently requested or core types of tasks?

   YES   NO   SOMETIMES   NOT SURE

2. Do you know how many hours your reports put in on average workdays and during average workweeks (including responding to emails and messages from managers and project partners)?

   YES   NO   SOMETIMES   NOT SURE

3. Do you know how often your reports complete an assignment in the amount of time you expected it to take?

   YES   NO   SOMETIMES   NOT SURE

4. Before assigning a new undertaking, do you ask your team members for realistic feedback regarding the amount of time it may take

them to complete that task?

YES   NO   SOMETIMES   NOT SURE

5. Before assigning a new undertaking, do you ask your reports for realistic feedback regarding the time that will be required to complete the amount of work *already* on their plates?

YES   NO   SOMETIMES   NOT SURE

6. If you ask for the feedback in items 4 and/ or 5 above, do you ask your team members which existing and new projects they see as top priorities?

YES   NO   SOMETIMES   NOT SURE

7. When you assign and *before your team member commits*, are you very specific about what *you* need done, while also eliciting your *team member's* estimate of the resources required, and other tasks that may need to be moved, in order to avoid capacity problems?

YES   NO   SOMETIMES   NOT SURE

8. Do you check in with your team members either daily or weekly (or both) for the status of the tasks you have assigned?

YES   NO   SOMETIMES   NOT SURE

9. Do you utilize brief status-check meetings (e.g., huddles) to uncover bottleneck issues

such as capacity overload?

YES   NO   SOMETIMES   NOT SURE

10. Do you (or does your company) promote the use of tech platforms such as Yammer and Facebook Workplace to help reduce the number of daily meetings, freeing up more time to focus on assignments and workloads?

YES   NO   SOMETIMES   NOT SURE

11. Do you help your reports to re-prioritize the tasks you have assigned?

YES   NO   SOMETIMES   NOT SURE

12. Do you make sure projects are well thought through so that you are not assigning and reassigning versions of the same project, thus creating double or triple work for your own reports?

YES   NO   SOMETIMES   NOT SURE

13. Do your reports proactively advise you when projects or assignments have hit (or are in danger of hitting) a capacity bottleneck?

YES   NO   SOMETIMES   NOT SURE

14. Do you routinely urge your team members to feel free to alert you ("No surprises!") to potential capacity issues?

YES   NO   SOMETIMES   NOT SURE

15. Do you routinely offer assistance to help resolve capacity issues via any or all of the

following: additional staff, support, resources, renegotiated deadlines?

YES   NO   SOMETIMES   NOT SURE

16. Does your company culture include a genuine interest in addressing capacity overload among its workforce?

YES   NO   SOMETIMES   NOT SURE

CHAPTER SEVEN

THE COMPETENCE/ CONFIDENCE CHALLENGE

If my bosses knew what I don't know, they never would have hired me for this job.

—Many of my clients

I've had any number of clients tell me, "If my bosses knew what I don't know, they never would have hired me for this job." People frequently feel, "I'm in way over my head; I'll just have to figure it out as I go." Nowadays, I hear all the time, even from top-level executives: "I'm being asked to do things I've never done before—things *no one* at my company has ever done before!"

And when performance and productivity break down, employers quickly move to assess the competence of their employees—too often, to pin blame. Think back to the story in Chapter One about one of my clients, a division head for a Midwest civil construction firm: Mark was perfectly competent for the many years he helped his boss, the CEO, build the business. But when Mark's CEO tied his hands by not enabling him to bring on and train new hires (resulting in a near-calamitous staffing snafu on a client job), Mark's performance review went south. His boss's feedback that Mark had "dropped the ball" was a stinging indictment of incompetence. Yet who, ultimately, was the culprit in that situation?

Now think about the enthusiastic team member who lobbies her manager for additional training to develop her expertise but is told, "There's no funding for additional training," or, "We don't have time to stop for training—we need to get this job done *now*."

Consider another team member brave enough to speak up and say, "I don't feel I'm the right person for this new post; I don't have the needed skills and I'm concerned that I won't be able to do the job properly."

And how about the job candidate who applies for a position in his skill area but is pressured into taking a position that needs to get filled first, one for which his competencies are not as well suited?

COMPETENCE AND PERFORMANCE: WHAT'S A MANAGER'S ROLE?

When it comes down to it, *who is responsible for ensuring that an employee has the competence to do the job?* Management guru Tom Peters, in his newest book, *The Excellence Dividend*,[35] states it well: "Your principal moral obligation as a leader is to develop the skill set of every one of the people in your charge … to the maximum extent of your abilities and consistent with their 'revolutionary' needs in the years ahead."

In other words, no matter how fast the world is changing, and how dramatically your company must change along with it, *you, the*

---

35   Tom Peters, *The Excellence Dividend: Meeting the Tech Tide with Work That Wows and Jobs That Last (New York: Random House, 2018).*

company leader and manager, are responsible for competence. If you are faced with incompetence, blame yourself for not:

- **Hiring** the right people.

- Providing them with the right **training.**

- **Tracking** their competency levels.

- **Casting** (or recasting) them in the roles in which they will shine.

- Effectively **integrating** their skills (plus valuable innate attributes) across the team and the various generations in your workplace.

Your job is to figure out what's required. If you can't, *you're* failing your workers; they're not failing *you.*

Film director Robert Altman was speaking of the movie industry when he noted the following, but his words apply to those who direct and manage in any industry: "The role of the director is to create a space where the actors and actresses can become more than they have ever been before, more than they ever dreamed of being." Make that your competence-and-confidence gold standard for all your team members, and you will help your company become more than you could possibly have imagined.

BEST PRACTICES: HIRING FOR ATTRIBUTES AS CORE COMPETENCIES

The competencies that Southwest Airlines[36] looks for most are not just acquired process skills, but attributes that no amount of training could instill.

36 Southwest Airlines was one of *Inc.'s 50 Best Places to Work in 2018.*

"We talk about hiring not for skills but three attributes," writes Julie Weber,[37] Southwest's vice president of people: "a warrior spirit (that is, a desire to excel, act with courage, persevere, and innovate); a servant's heart (the ability to put others first, treat everyone with respect, and proactively serve customers); and a fun-loving attitude (passion, joy, and an aversion to taking oneself too seriously)."

Southwest takes these core competencies so seriously that the company builds its interviewing methodology around detecting them. The airline uses behavioral interview questions to determine whether candidates possess those key attributes.

"Obviously, certain positions require specific skill sets. We're not going to hire a pilot who has a great attitude but can't fly a plane!" says Weber. But if it comes down to two equally qualified candidates, the individual demonstrating Southwest's core values will receive the offer. More importantly, "When we're faced with a qualified candidate who doesn't have the right values," says Weber, "we won't make an offer—no matter how long the job has gone unfilled." Southwest's three attributes are nonnegotiable competencies.

---

37   Julie Weber, "How Southwest Airlines Hires Such Dedicated People," *Harvard Business Review, December 2, 2015, https://hbr.org/2015/12/ how-southwest-airlines-hires-such-dedicated-people.*

THE COMPETENCE CHALLENGE: ASSESSING AT BREAKNECK SPEED

Today, managers not only have to assess their employees' capabilities prior to hiring them, they have to assess and reassess continually, rapidly, and effectively as job responsibilities mutate. And we're not just talking about the assessment of technical competency. Managers need also to assess their reports for:

- The **innate attributes** that will help them muster the confidence to tackle the challenges at hand.

- The **ability to keep learning** so that they can meet the challenges hurtling toward them, enhancing strengths and remediating weaker skill areas.

Keeping open reciprocal lines of inquiry and dialogue between managers and reports is the absolute best way to assess in an ongoing fashion. To support that effort, savvy managers and coaches utilize no end of tools, scorecards, interview techniques, and templates to:

- **Check** on all levels of competency.

- Ensure that team members' **hard and soft skills are fully aligned** with the core values of the organization and the company's culture.

- Ensure that **confidence levels** are high.

Some assessment tools (such as 360-degree assessments) are better suited to higher-level executives and company leaders; other tools are ideal for assessment of mid-level management. The point is, you are trying to get a clear snapshot of *why* your people are doing what they do. Ensuring accountability—the delivery of anticipated results—is always easier to achieve when you can glimpse your people from the inside and uncover what is engaging or thwarting them.

ASSESSMENT TOOLBOX SAMPLER

Below is a cross section of assessment tools and resources. Google any or all of the offerings below and use this list as a jumping-off point to discover even more; new entrants crop up daily.

- DISC personality test
- The Enneagram
- Hogan Assessments
- Holland Codes (occupational)
- Myers-Briggs Test and Personality Assessment
- Predictive Index
- The Productivity Test
- Rosenberg Self-Esteem Scale

COMPETENCE AND CASTING IN A WORLD OF MOVING-TARGET JOBS

When individuals are properly hired yet then fail or seem not to be competent, oftentimes they are cast in the wrong role or moved around after the fact, placed in a role in which they cannot succeed.

One of the reasons for miscasting is that today, jobs are moving targets. (How often, in fact, have *you* been hired or assigned to do one thing and then were asked to do numerous other things as well?) It happens all the time, because these days, as HR people like to say, job descriptions are "fluid." Management *expects* their positions to morph along the way as the business expands and changes moment by moment according to the needs of the marketplace and the world at large. To make matters worse, often an individual hired to do one job soon is not only performing a completely different role, but handling the original job *plus* the new one(s)—making the opportunities to master new competencies even harder to seize.

Thus, employees end up cast in jobs for which they are neither trained nor prepared; jobs they have no real enthusiasm for. Additionally, employees can end up under managers they don't mesh with well—bosses who erode their confidence and make it impossible for them to execute fully.

As companies are challenged to figure it out as they go along and reinvent themselves day by day, their leaders hope their workforce will be fully engaged in the journey into the unknown. The truth is, depending on the culture of the company and the skills of its managers, the experience can be an exciting ride for all, or a descent into futility.

But a company culture wherein managers are also coaches—directors who "create a space where the actors and actresses can become more than they have ever been before," returning to Altman's words—can make all the difference when it comes to the Competence C on the 7Cs checklist. In an exciting and challenging environment where your people can become more than they have been previously, the manager-as-coach is basically saying, "Yes, this is unknown territory for all of us. Like the starship *Enterprise*, we're all going where no one has gone before. But we're doing it together. It's going to a fascinating adventure, challenging and at times exhausting, but we're in it as a *team* and I'm here to help all along the way."

What an enticing scenario that would be for a brand-new millennial hire! Where she might have felt she was the only one who couldn't seem to keep up with things, she will now know that:

- You are there to help cast her in her most effective role.

- You are there to keep a two-way dialogue of inquiry and feedback going, to ensure there are few surprises along the way.

- You will help to equip her for whatever comes next.

NOT HIRING HIGH? TRAINING CAN MAKE THE DIFFERENCE

In smaller and family-owned companies, something else is often at play: company owners just don't want to pay enough money to hire the right person, so they routinely don't hire "high" enough for competency and confidence. With every check he writes, the CEO as business owner feels the dollars coming out of his pocket—and sometimes they are. Often, he's even working crazy hours to save himself from hiring people (highly competent people) he sees as too expensive. So he's employing *himself* to execute where his own competence level isn't high enough, or where he simply doesn't have the bandwidth to do the job needed.

When he does hire, he'll often hire people who are limited. He may hire people whose competency levels are acceptable for the business as it exists today but who he knows won't be able to grow with the business as he envisions it tomorrow. Or he'll hire those who have some experience but little confidence to excel. Frequently, such CEOs hire "affordable" people they already know are stretched beyond their capabilities, and then they expect them to magically stretch to new heights without training, certification, or development, let alone the drive to keep stretching.

Think about all the businesses, for example, that hire a bookkeeper who eventually becomes the controller. The controller then morphs into the company CFO—without the skills of a CFO. When serious financial challenges arise, the hard-dollar cost of that CFO's lack of expertise becomes huge.

And how many times have you come across an ineffectual sales manager who, while initially a perfectly good salesperson, should never have been promoted to sales manager, an entirely different function? His boss will tell you that she saved a bundle promoting the guy from within instead of paying the going rate to bring a top sales manager on board. Yet training or coaching could have dramatically altered this situation and others like it.

One of my clients, Christina, is the CEO of a $5 million niche real estate business: her company sells new residential construction to Americans relocating to Italy. Her agents are commission only, and she has very little outlay for sales and marketing management, which she has rolled into one function because she doesn't want to pay two large salaries for the two sets of business strengths.

But Christina has never been happy with her sales and marketing directors (there have been many). They have undoubtedly not worked out because the competencies required of a sales director are very different from those of someone with marketing expertise. Christina's dual hires have all been competent at one side of the dual job, not the other. Christina could, theoretically, handle the marketing function herself, but she'd rather travel in Italy while her sales and marketing director works from the United States. She also does not want to reduce her own income to pay for two separate but well-qualified directors. In the meantime, Christina continues to burn through sales and marketing directors, and her company sales are not growing (which would allow her to retire and/or sell the company). Instead, enterprise growth is stalled.

But "competency is the key here," I explained to Christina, when we recently launched our work together. "How often have you had a marketing and sales director who was equally good at both functions?" I asked her.

She admitted that had not yet happened. "When they're decent at managing the sales team, they fall down on the marketing," she complained. "Then when I get on them about the marketing, the sales side suffers and the marketing isn't even good enough to be worth it."

"What is that telling you?" I asked her.

"It's telling me that people don't know how to do their jobs!" she said, and then wondered aloud, "Am I asking too much?"

"Yes," I told her. "Too much for too little." Hiring a competent sales director with a strong background in sales team management would solve the sales side of Christina's dilemma, which she has agreed is her most urgent requisite. Then she could hire a less experienced (and much less expensive) individual with marketing talent and make available valuable and ongoing training to ensure competency. Both hires would be free to focus on their unique strengths and grow in their positions, making the company the ultimate beneficiary.

Most coaching clients—even CEOs—have to learn to step back so that they can see the bigger picture, connect the dots between the C or Cs that are the culprits, and their own behavior. Only then can they claim their prize. In this case, the leading C culprit is Competence. The behavior getting in the way is Christina's myopia about financial outlay (the Compensation C), plus her persistent misunderstanding about the elasticity of Capacity, yet another C. The prize is sales and marketing results that lead to growth, which will allow Christina's business to hum along smoothly while she continues to enjoy her life as a traveling entrepreneur.

SOFT-SKILLS TRAINING AT THE TOP

As an executive coach for some of the largest companies in the United States, I am often called in to provide the kind of training that helps an enterprise leader or senior-level manager to better balance his or her strengths and weaknesses. Frequently that involves helping really smart people develop better soft skills or emotional intelligence (EQ).

Recently, for instance, I was called in to work with a BioPharm leader who was heading up a high-level research team. I can't imagine an individual with higher levels of technical competence (and more impressive PhDs) than Jacob. And yet, the team was having trouble moving forward because managing people is not Jacob's strong suit; he's a scientist, and scientists are often introverts.

Without management skills, however, a team leader cannot effectively lead. Soft skills have everything to do with the 7Cs—the Cs we have already discussed and those we have yet to mine. Importantly, soft skills rely on the ability to keep two-way dialogue and inquiry flowing and ongoing, ensuring that team members are clear on their objectives, are free to speak up whenever needed, are encouraged to request what they need to achieve their tasks and goals, and are motivated and appreciated; never undermined by their own team leader. You would be amazed at just how common it is for people who have reached the heights of their careers (and org charts) to have developed lopsided job skills/soft skills competence. In such cases, coaching (or soft skills training) can have a positive impact that reverberates not just across the entire team but throughout the entire company as well.

ONGOING LEARNING FOR COMPETENCY IN A RAPIDLY CHANGING WORLD

Most companies are pretty good at assessing competency at point of hire. They want to know if an employee or a job candidate has the expertise and training to do the job required, and how well that individual might perform. To that end, companies often interview intensely, and test for skills before hiring.

Yet, how many companies promote a culture that advocates *ongoing* training and provides resources for it? Fast-growing enterprises (especially those with workforces reliant on millennial talent) tend to nurture such cultures more than conventional businesses do. Does the following sound familiar? "We're too busy to train. Besides, we don't have the budget to keep training people!" But think about how your *competition* may be preparing its workforce for its rapidly changing market. While the average retail store, for instance, spends eight hours on training,[38] The Container Store (on *Fortune*'s "100 Best Companies to Work For" list) spends two hundred hours training its people to be super competent. *Two hundred* hours!

Ongoing learning is all about helping people to be competent in their changing work, and thus confident that they can meet their ever-evolving challenges. No wonder it is the number one contributing factor in employee engagement! In fact, an astounding 87

---

38 According to the Friedman Group, a global retail consulting and training firm.

percent of millennials say that access to professional development or career-growth learning is key to the decision to join and stay with a company.[39] A smart boss tells his new millennial hires, "I can't guarantee you lifelong employment here, but I can guarantee you'll leave smarter. Wherever you go, you'll take knowledge and skills that will add value to your future." That learning advantage can often make up for a starting salary lower than your new hire may have anticipated.

COMPETENCE AND CONFIDENCE: TWO CS THAT GO HAND IN HAND

Confidence and the lack of it can affect anyone's competency levels, no matter the generation. What's more, given today's rate of change in the world and workplace, plus the speed with which job responsibilities and scope morph, it's not surprising that confidence issues abound. From CEOs on down, people are constantly moving into areas for which they do not yet have well-developed skill sets. They are continually having to learn on the fly. That means that most of us are working in our "discomfort zone" much of the time, and that does not build confidence. To put it plainly, it makes people feel that they are continually trying to achieve some sort of balance on exceedingly shaky ground. In fact, this section could rightly be called "The Three Cs That Go Hand in Hand: Competence, Confidence, and *Change.*"

This is where your millennials can shine, for they often breeze into a change-driven workplace undaunted by any transmutation. Raised in an era of powerful yet generally positive disruption, they

---

39 "2017 Employee Engagement & Loyalty Statistics," Access Perks, August 28, 2017, https://blog.accessperks.com/2017-employee-engagement-loyalty-statistics.

are the least change-averse of all the generations. Change is stimulating to them. They actually dread doing the same thing over and over.

Still, millennials often face a bizarre competence/confidence predicament: they do not want to be held back from performing at high levels and advancing at a rapid rate, yet they often have little confidence in their ability to navigate the workplace without a strong mentor to guide them. This paradoxical tug-of-war between (sometimes overinflated) competence and (at times, wobbly) confidence is thought to stem from upbringing: many millennials were raised to believe that they are exceptional, yet their parents remained close at hand to relentlessly advise and guide. The subliminal message was: you are special and can do *anything*—with my help. Many millennials, in fact, enter the working world while still living at home, unlike their boomer parents who were out of the house and on their own by eighteen. Not surprisingly, the workplace can present a very real shock for millennials. "I thought I was special and could achieve anything. So how come I can't ace this job?"

MANAGING FOR COMPETENCE AND CONFIDENCE

A great manager helps her people to believe in themselves—to believe that they can accomplish great things. Some of the best managers I have ever encountered inspired more than accountability: they inspired people to do things they never believed they could do. In short, a great manager is someone who *builds* confidence in people, and strives never to erode it—for she knows that her people are her greatest resource.

Great managers build confidence in their people the way great parents do: one baby step at a time, "chunking" tasks to make them achievable, not insurmountable. Like effective parents, great managers utilize what's called PICs—positive, immediate, certain consequences—to motivate their charges.[40] Great managers set doable (SMART) goals, and applaud their people for achieving them. Then they repeat the process, stretching just a bit each time, to build pride in accomplishment.

Likewise, a manager who seeks to establish clarity through inquiry and dialogue also has a greater chance of building confidence, because *confidence is relative to the request*. For instance, if I said, "Can you take a walk around the park?" you'd say, "No problem." And if I said, "Could you take a half-mile walk?" you'd probably say, "Sure." But if I asked you take a hundred-mile walk with me, you'd doubtless say, "I'm not quite ready for that!"

Looking at past generations, it's curious to see how earlier generations of both parents and managers believed that clarity and baby steps were not the way to go—tough love was the route to confidence: keep knocking 'em down and see if they get up, or throw them in the water and let them figure out how to swim. Parents of millennials must have resented that kind of upbringing so much that they opted to instill confidence through constant verbal reassurance—and then made sure their kids made the grade by stepping in to meet their challenges for them.

One of my clients, Dan, who runs a $50-million organization with twenty people reporting to him, came to me with complaints about his boss, who was constantly eroding his confidence by stepping in, and stepping all over him.

---

40   PICs constitute a methodology presented by Aubrey Daniels, "the father of performance management," who maintained in his book *Bringing Out the Best in People (New York: McGraw-Hill, 1994)* that the brain actually changes when people and animals know that a specific behavior will be followed by a response behavior. Positive, immediate, certain responses reinforce behaviors.

"I needed to promote three of my people to manager spots to better control our workload," he reported, "but my boss stepped in and told me I could only promote one, so we're still not functioning as we could be." To top it off, he added, his boss had just argued with him about attending a workshop. "I can't get him to think strategically about where we're going and how we're going to get there, but he's micromanaging me about spending fifty bucks on a seminar," he groaned.

MENTORING FOR COMPETENCE AND CONFIDENCE

Some people are born managers, and some people have to work exceptionally hard at managing even adequately. In the meantime, new hires—especially millennials—often struggle with managers who are struggling as well. And yet it is critical that new hires develop confidence on the job in order to remain engaged. That's where a mentor can make a remarkable difference. According to a study by the Association for Talent Development, 75 percent of top executives say a mentor somewhere along the way was instrumental in helping them develop the confidence to achieve their current position.[41]

Early on, especially, new reports need an agent of as many of the 7Cs as possible: someone who represents the company *Culture* at its best, who is there to *Clarify* what seems ambiguous or intimidating, who can help gauge *Capacity* at eye level, who can assist in developing *Competence* and thus *Confidence*, and who demonstrates that the company is *Committed* to the development of its new hire because it truly cares.

41　ADT Research, "Mentoring Matters: Developing Talent With Formal Mentoring Programs," Association for Talent Development, November 2017, https://www.td.org/research-reports/mentoring-matters-developing-talent-with-formal-mentoring-programs.

Think of the power behind that kind of jumpstart for new hires. Think of the vast benefits to an organization that could engage, support, inspire, and fully develop their people to such a degree. And yet, we all know that time is at a premium everywhere, especially for managers. Still, the benefits of mentoring are now so clear that according to recent coverage in *The Wall Street Journal,* 70 percent of Fortune 500 companies have created mentoring programs wherein new hires are teamed with company veterans to help them develop their job skills, leadership abilities, and self-assurance.[42] Some of the best mentorship programs as of 2018 are: Boeing, Caterpillar, Deloitte, General Electric, Google, Intel, KPMG, Liberty Mutual, McGraw-Hill, Sodexo, Spectrum, and Zynga.

"I've gotten zero mentoring from my boss," one of my clients, Dan, admitted to me recently. He went on to say that he saw a "tremendous need for learning and mentoring at every single level" of his organization. "The only training I've received as a leader since I came to work at my company is the coaching experience I have with you!" he laughed. Happily, Dan is a fast learner who has rapidly internalized the 7Cs and is using what he has learned to build a team of reports who are both highly skilled, well appreciated, and thus deservedly confident.

TAKE ACTION: BE A CONFIDENCE BUILDER, NOT BREAKER

To make sure you are working on your confidence-building skills instead of feeding an unconscious

---

42 Toddi Gutner, "Finding Anchors in the Storm: Mentors," *The Wall Street Journal, last modified January 27, 2009, https://www.wsj.com/articles/ SB123301451869117603.*

tendency to erode others' confidence, try these simple behavior modification techniques:

Snap a rubber band on your wrist. Every time you hear yourself speaking in a confidence-eroding manner ("Why did you do that?" "Do I have to tell you how to do everything?" "I'll get Joe to do it; he'll be able to handle this"), snap the band against the inside of your wrist to associate your own pain with causing pain to another person, and to change unwanted behavior.

Ask for a do-over. Instead of letting someone walk out of your office after you have behaved in a confidence-eroding way, call the individual back in and apologize in a straightforward manner. "Sorry about that, Jen. That was not at all what I meant to say. Let's try this again: What's going on, and how can I help?"

Practice your PICs. Did someone just do a great job? Deliver the goods you were hoping for? React with PICs—positive, immediate, certain consequences (consequences that you present each and every time). Try a group email that applauds and rewards: "Just wanted you all to know that Nora's team nailed their sales goals for March, and we owe them a big vote of thanks for working so hard to make those numbers in this super-tough economy. We know it's been a real challenge for everyone. Kudos to Nora, Sam, Rashida, Arne, and Ben. A hundred bucks goes to each of their designated causes/charities!"

CHAPTER EIGHT

COMMITMENT: THE HEART OF THE MATTER

Successful people become great leaders when they learn to shift the focus from themselves to others.

—Marshall Goldsmith, author of *What Got You Here Won't Get You There: How Successful People Become Even More Successful*

As a business leader coach, one of the toughest concepts to get across is that of commitment reciprocity. Every client wants to know why so many company employees can't fully deliver on the promise to "just do their job." They want to know why it has become harder and harder for employees to keep their commitments to their employers and be fully accountable. What so many managers—even those at the highest corporate levels—do not grasp is that their workers are feeling the exact same way.

When Jessica came on board as head of US marketing for a leading appliance maker, she was thrilled. She was excited to dig in and wow her boss with the kind of dedication and innovation the company had been looking for ever since her predecessor had announced his departure (he defected to a competitor). Her husband laughingly told her that during her first months on the job, her feet barely touched the ground—even with the long hours, limited sleep, and time away from their home. Before Jessica took the new post, the couple had thoughtfully discussed the many sacrifices they would be making with the advent of her new challenges. Both were prepared to make the needed concessions for a position that would bring Jessica greater job satisfaction, a sizable increase in salary, and the realization of career goals that she had only dreamt about.

A little under three years later, after a full twelve months of feeling mentally and emotionally "checked out," Jessica was ready to hand in her resignation, and her boss knew it. The trouble was, Jessica's boss—who held one of the most senior posts in the company—was at a loss to understand what her issues were. In fact, he had never been certain why the *previous* head of marketing had been so open to recruitment away from the firm. He simply assumed it was a money issue. Jessica could have told him otherwise.

"I kept every commitment I made to this company, and then some," she declared. "I took marketing to a whole new level, which dramatically boosted sales revenue; I brought in some of the best talent in the industry; and I helped us win industry awards that weren't even on the radar when I came on board. There has been no personal sacrifice I have not willingly and unflinchingly made for this company," she insisted, "and my boss knows it."

COMMITMENT: THE HEART OF THE MATTER, THE TOUGHEST FIX

So what was the problem? "I know this sounds silly," Jessica admitted, "but I don't think he appreciates any of it. We've never even had a lunch together, and sometimes I get the feeling he can't remember my last name!" On the other hand, she pointed out, he had no trouble calling her out in front of colleagues and agency partners when something displeased him. "The culture here is 'What have you done for me lately?' and after almost three years, I'd rather work for less money someplace where my work actually means something. I'd like to work where people care about other people—even just a little bit!"

Jessica's story isn't new. In fact, in the age of millennials, when employees seek purpose and personal gratification in their work more than ever, this scenario has become commonplace. Somewhere between onboarding and the point where they "check out" and became thoroughly disengaged, something happens to many workers in any strata of any organization. When a staff member is no longer performing, a manager can run through the toolbox of Cs to pinpoint the root or roots of the issue. Is it Clarity or Capacity? The manager can certainly address those problems with appropriate changes. If Competence is the culprit, the manager can respond with training, mentoring, or recasting.

Often, though, "checking out" has everything to do with the C of Commitment—the absence of a *manager's* commitment to his or her employee.[43] This lack of commitment is most often characterized by the lack of caring that is the underpinning of commitment. The truth is, once an employee senses that the manager (and, by extension, the company) does not care about him and is not committed to his well-being or success within the organization, his heart has been lost. That's because when we're talking about commitment, what we're really talking about is engaging the heart. Unlike the Cs of Clarity, Capacity, or even Competence, the C of Commitment (meaning

---

43   Patrick Lencioni speaks of this in his landmark book *The Five Dysfunctions of a Team: A Leadership Fable (San Francisco: Jossey-Bass, 2002).*

reciprocal commitment: you don't care about me, so why should I care about you?) is mighty hard to turn around. After all, you've lost the heart of your worker.

This is why so many top companies measure employee engagement on a regular basis and try to address issues promptly. These companies understand that engagement has everything to do with feeling appreciated and respected by one's manager and company. After all, the quickest way to lose an employee's heart is to ignore the good stuff that individual does, take it for granted, and be quick to criticize mistakes. Great leaders help their people go home feeling great about themselves. Their employees feel great because their work is acknowledged and appreciated on a consistent basis, and because what they care about (family, community, work/life balance) matters to their boss, too.

> ## THE QUICKEST WAY TO LOSE AN EMPLOYEE'S HEART IS TO IGNORE THE GOOD STUFF THAT INDIVIDUAL DOES, TAKE IT FOR GRANTED, AND BE QUICK TO CRITICIZE MISTAKES.

Unhappily, losing one heart is only the beginning of a manager's—and thus a company's—problems. Lose one heart and you've also lost that individual's creativity and "spark." Then things snowball as your employee veers toward passive-aggressiveness, stops doing what she is expected to do, starts looking for a new job, and engages in water cooler conversations with anyone who will listen to her gripe about how awful her boss is. Soon, news of your unfeeling company hits cyberspace on websites such as Glassdoor: "This place is terrible. They don't care about people. They don't care about me. They don't take care of their employees. Don't work here!" Employee engagement begins to dip, while turnover rates suddenly move upward and performance falters.[44]

TWENTY-FIRST CENTURY PEOPLE WANT TO FEEL GOOD ABOUT THEMSELVES

Unless a manager is purposely abusive (and unfortunately, callous managers still crop up here and there), unfeeling managers seldom realize that *when people feel lousy at work, their natural instinct will be to feel better as soon as possible.* Bob Cratchit may have toiled in endless deprivation for Ebenezer Scrooge when expectations for nineteenth century clerks were generally dismal everywhere. Today, however, across developed nations, twenty-first century human beings seek happiness. Those who work in organizations not reciprocally committed to them quickly realize their job is not the right job for them. Unfortunately, because so few bosses are actually trained to be good leaders, there is still a glut of bosses out there in the marketplace who come across as uncaring and uncommitted.

The equation is simple: Do you want committed workers who care about their team, their boss, and their company? You've got to be committed to *them* and care about *them*, too.

But, you say, we care about our people—we pay well and offer excellent health benefits and vacation pay. Certainly there is no disputing the importance of appropriate compensation and benefits, especially today, when competition for talent is intense and incoming generations of workers demonstrate salary and benefits expectations

---

44 Recommended reading on this kind of downward spiraling: Susan Scott, *Fierce Conversations (New York: Penguin Group, 2002);* Kerry Patterson, Joseph Grenny, Ron McMillan, and Al Switzler, *Crucial Confrontations (*New York: McGraw-Hill, 2004).

many companies have never before encountered. Yet caring and commitment cannot stop at HR benefits policy. An organization and its culture must encourage all of its managers to personally care about workers and commit to their well-being, just as caring and commitment to the company is anticipated of all employees.[45]

COMMITMENT RECIPROCITY AND SUCCESS

In *The Seven Spiritual Laws of Success: A Practical Guide to the Fulfillment of Your Dreams*,[46] Deepak Chopra, bestselling author and torchbearer of the New Age movement, describes the law of reciprocity. This very basic law essentially says, "Give what you want to receive. Don't do it *because* you want to receive that same thing, but understand that giving begets receiving." Do you want to receive love? Be loving. Want to receive commitment? Demonstrate your own commitment. Want to receive caring? Then *you* must care. And if you hope to receive appreciation, you must appreciate others, too. In other words: give the things you most want to receive, because the act itself creates an imbalance in the universe that begs balancing. In Japanese culture, if you give someone a gift, that person will understand an obligation to give you a gift back. Can that obligation feel uncomfortable at times? Yes; but the law of reciprocity explains how the world at large tends to reciprocate, just as the law of gravity demonstrates that things that are dropped tend to fall.

Even so, commitment reciprocity hasn't thrived in the workplace. Any reciprocity that does exist is often relegated to HR, which in

---

45   This concept is explored in depth in Simon Sinek, *Start with Why: How Great Leaders Inspire Everyone to Take Action*. London: Portfolio (Penguin Books), 2009.

46   Deepak Chopra, *The Seven Spiritual Laws of Success: A Practical Guide to the Fulfillment of Your Dreams* (Novato, CA: New World Library/Amber-Allen Publishing, 1994).

itself defies "humanness" (even though human resources has "human" right there in its name). Yet, if you're interested in accountability, the laws of the universe will still prevail. So, if you've lost the heart of your people—that is, if they've stopped caring about you (their boss) and thus the company as a whole—then they certainly can't be committed to delivering what they should. And that's a direct route to nonaccountability.

An important note here: if you believe that "motivating" your people is more directly related to employee accountability than is commitment reciprocity, it's time to take a hard look at the age-old theory behind motivating others—carrots and sticks.

Simply stated, carrots and sticks[47] are ineffective. The reason is simple: to hold out carrots (rewards) or sticks (punishment), a boss must be hovering somewhere nearby, creating incentives or else cracking a whip. The sense is that without directed motivation or repercussion, things will pretty much go to hell in a handbasket. On the other hand, *inspiring* accountability is a matter of having all your Cs in place; commitment and caring figuring prominently in the mix. When employees have what they need to be successful, are fully engaged in their work, and their hearts are with boss and enterprise, no motivating efforts are needed; employees are self-motivated A-players thriving in a meritocracy, and success is self-perpetuating.

Indeed, Best Places to Work companies don't need sticks and carrots; their internal commitments to their employees virtually guarantee engagement, accountability, and success. It had to have been a fully engaged and energized Apple employee, for instance, who came up with the idea of offering free classes at Apple stores, to help customers love their tech products and discover uses in all

---

47   Recommended reading: Paul L. Marciano, *Carrots and Sticks Don't Work (New York: McGraw-Hill Education, 2010).*

corners of their lives. Recently, when I stumbled onto the classes in my local Apple store (after an employee eagerly replaced an under-performing battery, gratis), I asked, "Why do you guys offer so many free classes?" "We really *care* about our users and we want them to feel connected to our community!" was the response. Only an employee whose heart is thoroughly engaged can be so clearly excited and enthusiastic about his customers. The fact is, caring about your workers is the best route to the success of the enterprise.

> THE FACT IS, CARING ABOUT YOUR WORKERS IS THE BEST ROUTE TO THE SUCCESS OF THE ENTERPRISE.

enterprise. Your people are your most important resource *and* they are the face your company presents to your public.

Certainly, if your employees have already lost heart, the fix isn't easy, because it needs to start with you, the manager or company leader. It's much easier to hand off your own commitment work to HR. But HR isn't a human being, and humans need to feel connected to other humans or they disengage.

CONNECTING IN A WORLD WITH NO TIME: FOUR FIXES

In my coaching work with company leaders, the two phrases I hear most are: "I want to connect with my people, but there's just no time for that anymore!" Or, worse, "I'm paying them to do a job; I don't *need* to know anything else about them!" Yes, as businesses get flatter and leaner, executives can be stretched to the breaking point. There's no question that one of the biggest conundrums busy top executives face is the fact that they need a 100 percent commitment from each of their people, while they cannot reciprocate with anything close to that.

A manager's typical complaint sounds like this: "Half the time, I can't even remember who has kids and who doesn't, whose parent is living at home, or whose spouse has just flown the coop. And I certainly don't know who is about to celebrate a birthday." Finessing all of these details seems impossible in this day and age. Still, the negative impact of seeming not to know anything about an individual working closely with you is great; it sends a clear signal that, true or not, you don't care to know the human being you expect to care about *you* and *your* needs. There are, however, ways around this dilemma.

Not long ago I was working with Kevin, who owns a business that will generate more than $100 million in revenue this year. Things weren't always looking up for his company, however; at one point, disengagement was a very real issue, even at the topmost levels. My surveys of his teams and discussions with them revealed that while his people came on board with a genuine desire to serve Kevin and the company well, sooner or later each team member experienced a certain level of detachment. Though the company employed hundreds, many of its workers also had regular interactions with Kevin's teams. And so there was a real danger of the top-level team disengagement spreading.

Unfortunately, Kevin was not a people person, and his preoccupied demeanor was seriously off-putting to his own team. In his defense, he felt as though he worked forty-eight-hour days to keep his company moving forward. Yet, I suspected that his people felt that way too, and would feel more connected to him—and to their own reports—if he acknowledged them as human beings with families and lives outside of the workplace.

I suggested that we conduct a confidential employee survey of his team members to open up a dialogue and launch a process of real inquiry. In that way, Kevin could get a better sense of what his people were feeling. (This would be the first of many surveys; the more frequently team members are polled, the more communication with them is opened and the less likely their "heart" is lost.) I met with Kevin's team members, also confidentially, to encourage honest feedback and enable them to air their grievances to someone who could help their boss institute needed change. I also asked Kevin to step in more often on daily huddles, to increase his opportunities to connect with his people.

Importantly, I rolled out three simple fixes that would help Kevin regain the trust and connection to his team by showing that he cared about them and was committed to their well-being in his company. In turn, the increased commitment and connectedness his leadership team members felt from their boss would be modeled and passed along to their own teams—and so forth and so on.

Fix No. 1—Hire your alter ego. First, because Kevin could not remember his team members' birthdays, anniversaries, kids' names, favorite pastimes, or much else about their personal lives,[48] I convinced him to hire an executive assistant whose job it would be to help advance the human side of the CEO. Initially, Kevin balked at the expense for a right hand, a hire that seemed self-indulgent and would incur expense for such a "touchy-feely" purpose.

But, "You need an alter ego," I insisted. "Someone who makes you look good to the team. You've got hundreds of people working for you, and somebody who is an extension of you can send a birthday and anniversary card to every one of them and, prior to meetings

---

48 Recommended reading about the importance of this: Harvey MacKay, *Dig Your Well Before You're Thirsty (New York: Doubleday, 1997)*.

and interactions, can remind you to ask how their children or elderly parents are doing."

"I'm not the president of the United States!" Kevin protested. Then I shared that years ago, for my own company, I had hired the same kind of personal assistant. I had realized that, as president of my own firm, I simply didn't have the bandwidth to carry out the many human tasks that would help me connect to my team members. I greatly valued them, yet I could sense that I was disappointing them. My new assistant made me look good, because my people always felt acknowledged and appreciated by me.

Fix No. 2—Calendar regular wandering. I advised Kevin to spend time each day wandering around his company offices and noting the good work his people were doing, or talking to his managers to find out what *their* people were doing well. More than urge him to get into the habit of wandering, I asked Kevin to calendar his wandering time. It could be ten minutes to pop in on team members, or forty minutes to sit and chat here and there. My own Gazelles training suggests speaking informally with at least two employees per week, any valuable feedback to be offered up at weekly team meetings. But, "Build it into each day and every week," I explained, "or it won't happen."

Importantly, I wanted him to hear firsthand the stories that would filter up to him from his middle managers. "Every single week, tell them that you are there to hear about someone who works for them who did something above and beyond; something that either was great for the company or consistent with the core values of the business. If you don't seek out those stories," I warned him, "they will never filter up to you, and they will never filter up to your managers, either."

I pointed out that not wandering mimics the worst problems we face in our lives at home. Busy executives who do not calendar time for their children's important school and life events, for instance, eventually find themselves with strangers for offspring. And anyone can relate to spouses who leave their successful mates (or threaten to) because everything made it onto the daily calendar except time together. "It's exactly the same at work," I declared. The only difference is, it's your employees walking out the door—and they'll walk right over to your competition."

Fix No. 3—Acknowledge and praise. I asked Kevin to make sure to locate the sources of positive stories, acknowledge the work of those employees, and deliver his own personal appreciation as soon as possible—preferably the same day the news reached him, so that his pleasure in the accomplishment was palpable and genuine. Even a simple "Hey, I heard that you did a great job the other day with _____! Thanks so much for your work on behalf of the company."

Whole Foods managers, for instance, demonstrate and thus model just these types of consistent management behaviors to ensure that employees receive recognition and appreciation wherever it is earned. Managers work hard to stay connected to their employees, keeping reciprocal commitment coursing through the arteries of the enterprise daily.

Don't think demonstrating management commitment makes that much of a difference? I recall, years back, walking into the office of a senior executive I was coaching. Though I have long ago forgotten which executive or company it was (let's call him Joe), I'll never forget that on the wall near his desk was a framed handwritten letter from his boss that read, "Dear Joe, thanks so much for your extraordinary effort on this project. It made all the difference in the world. I really appreciate you." It was signed by his boss, and he told me that this letter meant more to him than any other in all his years of business.

Not surprisingly, countless studies[49] over many years have revealed that people work for much more than money: they work for acknowledgment, appreciation, and fulfillment. In addition, they're more likely to "go the extra mile" for recognition and appreciation than they are for money. So, assuming that compensation, title, and advancement have been appropriately matched to productivity, a great manager also lets her people know that she sees how hard they work for her, appreciates it, and is committed to keeping them happy in their jobs. That is the most powerful way to stay connected to employees and prevent detachment from manager and company. At the same time, such behavior models the most desirable cultural behavior for the entire enterprise.

To reinforce that his people are not invisible "working units" to him, I asked Kevin to always offer five bits of praise for every criticism he meted out to each team member or employee—a five-to-one ratio of "You did this right" vs. "You did this wrong." Further, I explained

---

49   Scads of recent articles and studies support the notion that people work for more than money: Victor Lipman, "New Employee Study Shows Recognition Matters More Than Money," Psychology Today, June 13, 2013, https://www.psychologytoday.com/us/blog/mind-the-manager/201306/new-employee-study-shows-recognition-matters-more-money; Donna Gray, "The Power of Recognition and Appreciation in Business," In Business, January 23, 2013, https://www.ibmadison.com/Blogger/The-Gray-Area/January-2013/The-power-of-recognition-and-appreciation-in-business/; Merge Gupta-Sunderji, "Why Money Is Not an Employee Motivator," The Globe and Mail, January 30, 2017, https://www.theglobeandmail.com/report-on-business/careers/leadership-lab/why-money-is-not-an-employee-motivator/article33755286/; Clare Hamilton, "People Work for Money—But Go the Extra Mile for Praise, Recognition and Rewards," LinkedIn, July 12, 2017, https://www.linkedin.com/pulse/people-work-money-go-extra-mile-praise-recognition-rewards-hamilton/.

that feedback must be frequent, to keep connections strong. Importantly, it should be immediate, specific, and *always* sincere.

His people, I stressed, should always know how he feels about them, and there should be no surprises; no one should ever be blindsided by being fired, for instance. That kind of surprise sprays shrapnel across an entire organization and undermines forged connections everywhere.

Fix No. 4—Institute skip-level and all-hands meetings. I suggested Kevin get to know, and interface with, the people who *work for* the people who report to him, via skip-level and all-hands meetings. I urged him to ask open-ended (not yes/no) questions and *listen*. I explained that the best way to demonstrate caring is to engage with people and listen to them and take what they have to say seriously. The purpose of skip-level and all-hands meetings is not to make announcements or tell people what to do, it's to hear what they *think* and get a good sense of who they are.

So, wander. Listen. Acknowledge, thank, and appreciate through words, emails, notes, *anything*. And hire someone to help you stay connected if you don't have enough time to recognize the life details of the human beings who help create your success. Small things *do* make a difference.

BEYOND COMMITMENT: SACRIFICE AND LOYALTY

Do you expect your people to make sacrifices for the team? While managing team members can be largely tactical ("Here's a job. Get it done.") oftentimes it's "Get it done with less resources than you need, faster than you can." That instantly sets up a tension: You expect sacrifices and loyalty from your team. So, what can they expect reciprocally from *you*?

There are only a few reasons people will make personal sacrifices, and money may be near the bottom of the list. While money can be a powerful motivator, it is an expensive one, and it does not tend to inspire *consistent* levels of energy, creativity, and resourcefulness. Then, too, its impact can evaporate quickly in the face of job misery.

The other two drivers are (a) fear and (b) desire. Workers either make personal sacrifices because they're (a) afraid of the consequences if they don't, or (b) because they really care about achieving for their team, company, boss, or all three. Unquestionably, fear is an effective motivator ("We might lose this account if we don't all pull together"), but it has a short shelf life. Desire, however, is a powerful motivator, because it has no shelf life at all. As Napoleon said: "A soldier will fight long and hard for a bit of *colored ribbon.*"

I've certainly seen examples of situations where workers will consistently make personal sacrifices (working late, forgoing a family vacation or event) and

EMPLOYEES WHO SACRIFICE FOR THEIR BOSSES AND COMPANIES FEEL CONNECTED TO SOMETHING THAT IS BIGGER THAN THEMSELVES.

even work for less than full compensation to achieve their "bit of colored ribbon." That's not because of tactical management; it's because they feel a very real sense of connection to their manager, team, or company.

In fact, the colored ribbon motivation is one reason why working in teams is so effective: it sets up a natural, healthy competitive spirit—as long as the company culture rewards teams that support their fellow teams for the good of the enterprise.

Simply put, employees who sacrifice for their bosses and companies feel connected to something that is bigger than themselves. They are aligned with the mission, vision, and values of the company and its culture, which is reinforced at every turn. Moreover:

- They do not feel that goals set by their managers are arbitrary or unobtainable.

- Their company culture is one in which they feel safe to speak their minds and ask for what they need.

- They know that mistakes are seen as a willingness to push envelopes and are not punished.

- Their managers understand the importance of casting (and recasting) their people to find their best roles.

- They feel "known" by their managers and peers, and do not feel invisible or as though they are "labor units." They feel a sense of partnership with their manager—that "We're in this together trying to accomplish goals that we agree are important."

In short, they experience caring and commitment from their employers, which can forge a bond of loyalty that moves them even beyond accountability. Have you known people who will follow their managers to the next job and the next? Have you wondered how that kind of connection is formed? I know a manager whose key team members have worked with him at three different jobs. When he moves, they move. He told me simply, "Their loyalty to me has everything to do with how I treat them."

ARE YOU A COMMITTED MANAGER? TWENTY-FIVE TELLTALE SIGNS YOU NEED HELP

We all like to believe we are caring managers, but here is your chance to be truly honest and solve serious problems by working on your Commitment C. Answer each question as best you can. There is no cumulative score here, but paying attention to each "true" item will provide you with an opportunity to move closer to mutually rewarding employee-manager relationships and the levels of accountability you have been seeking.

1. Employee engagement in your area is low and turnover is high.

    TRUE   FALSE   NOT SURE

2. You don't believe that people must be acknowledged or praised for their good work; good work is expected of them.

    TRUE   FALSE   NOT SURE

3. You believe (and may have stated) something like: "We are here to make money, and my part is that I pay my people a salary." Or "We don't need to coddle them. We don't need to pat them on the back. Their check is their reward." Or "Why offer incentives? If they

don't want to do the work I assign them, I'll fire them and find someone else."

TRUE   FALSE   NOT SURE

4. You see employee benefits and options such as flextime, working from home, half-day Fridays, and paternity leave for new fathers as something the company might offer to remain competitive in attracting job candidates, not necessarily as a demonstration of how much the company "cares" about its employees.

TRUE   FALSE   NOT SURE

5. Much as you might like to, you don't have the time to stop and chat informally with team members or workers. That would take you away from your own important work for the company.

TRUE   FALSE   NOT SURE

6. You believe that keeping business and personal information separate in the workplace is good practice. You don't want to know about your employees' family members, special occasions (birthdays, anniversaries, etc.), special circumstances (single mother, spouse with medical bills, elderly parent to support, etc.), and outside commitments (coaching children's sports, attending important spouse and children's events,

family vacations, community commitments, etc.).

TRUE   FALSE   NOT SURE

7. You have been told by family members and close friends that when people speak with you about their feelings, you are not fully listening or engaged.

TRUE   FALSE   NOT SURE

8. When you become aware of an employee's personal need to rely on job and paycheck (e.g., single mother, spouse with medical bills, elderly parent to support), you know that you have a dependent employee who you can rely on to do a good job and not jump ship.

TRUE   FALSE   NOT SURE

9. When one of your team members is willing to take on extra work, work late, or make other sacrifices to demonstrate his or her commitment to you and the company, you know you can go to this individual as your "go-to" person to step up to the plate whenever you need a pinch hitter.

TRUE   FALSE   NOT SURE

10. Even though it may have been unintentional on your part, there have been times you have caused your team members such high levels

of stress that you couldn't help but notice they were suffering under the strain. While you felt uncomfortable about causing pain, you did not speak to them about it.

TRUE   FALSE   NOT SURE

11. You have been told that when it comes to your reports and employees in general, you are short on praise and long on criticism. But you favor "time-honored" management techniques and believe that pointing out errors and shortcomings is generally more constructive than what you see as gratuitous praise.

TRUE   FALSE   NOT SURE

12. In your time-constrained work environment, you do not feel the need to deliver ongoing performance feedback to your team members. Your motto is closer to "I'll let you know when you're not doing something right. If you don't hear from me, things are fine."

TRUE   FALSE   NOT SURE

13. You've heard of studies indicating that most employees disengage or leave jobs because of their boss. You believe that if an employee leaves because of you or your management style, that employee was too thin skinned to offer real value to the company anyway.

TRUE   FALSE   NOT SURE

14. When team members or employees proactively contribute "company culture" ideas such as company or group sports events, themed days, working for community endeavors or charitable organizations, and so on, you are likely to disregard or put off the suggestions and see them as disruptions to the important work of the company.

TRUE   FALSE   NOT SURE

15. You do not believe that it is your responsibility (or that of your managers) to provide training, coaching, and development opportunities to expose people to new knowledge, stimulate learning, or help them become better leaders.

TRUE   FALSE   NOT SURE

16. You are not in favor of investing in an improved work environment simply because it is more conducive to "employee happiness and well-being" or because it helps to meet millennials' needs (e.g., added perks and life conveniences, increased space, employee lounges, updated cafeteria and snack facilities, day care facilities, private pumping stations for new mothers, new office furnishings, specialized furnishings such as height-adjustable desks, sundecks, workout rooms).

TRUE   FALSE   NOT SURE

17. When you find a team member who does not refuse a "grunt work" assignment (set up team barbecues, order tickets to events, arrange to have the copier fixed), you assign them such tasks over and over again even if (a) the tasks do not fit their job description, (b) their function is a good deal higher up on the org chart, or (c) the assignment could be construed as gender or race bias (for example, assigning such tasks to a female marketing director who is the only non-male on your team).

TRUE   FALSE   NOT SURE

18. You realize that in finding an individual who continually agrees to go "above and beyond" for you and the team, you have handed off more and more work to that person and have become dependent on that individual's extraordinary commitment to you and the team. Your dependence on that individual makes you uncomfortable.

TRUE   FALSE   NOT SURE

19. Given the choice of hiring for skill versus hiring for attitude, you will always choose skill while placing a lower value on attitude. (This question does not necessarily apply to brain surgery or rocket science.)

TRUE   FALSE   NOT SURE

20. You would never admit it publicly, but you do not enjoy managing people and handling "people issues." You sometimes look forward to a world where most of your reports will be artificially intelligent (AI) with no feelings and issues to deal with, and workdays will not be disrupted by human concerns.

TRUE   FALSE   NOT SURE

21. You have never instituted an employee engagement survey to find out how your people feel about working for you and the company.

TRUE   FALSE   NOT SURE

22. You were directed to institute an employee engagement survey to find out how your people feel about working for you and the company, but you have never done anything with the results.

TRUE   FALSE   NOT SURE

23. You have never seriously examined the company cultures of Best Places to Work winners such as Apple, Google, Salesforce, Southwest Airlines, and so on to get ideas for effective ways to forge improved recipro-

cal commitment and caring within your own organization or group.

TRUE   FALSE   NOT SURE

24. You have never personally visited websites such as Glassdoor and Indeed to see if your own organization's employees feel that their company and its leaders and managers care about them and are committed to them in ways that are important to them. (Those needs might include work/life balance, professional development, employee benefits, career guidance, and so on.)

TRUE   FALSE   NOT SURE

25. You are genuinely concerned about employee or team member accountability but have not seriously considered that your ability to *inspire* high levels of job performance may be directly related to—or at least significantly improved by—your own level of commitment to your people.

TRUE   FALSE   NOT SURE

TAKE ACTION: FIVE REFLECTIONS FOR COMMITMENT TURNAROUND

Take time to reflect on your answers to the questions above, and then ask yourself the following questions:

1. When it comes to our workforce, what measures has our company instituted over time to build or reinforce our levels of commitment to and caring about employees?

2. What specific commitment and caring efforts have I, as a company leader or manager, consistently demonstrated toward employees?

3. What five steps could I personally take to consistently forge reciprocal commitment and caring among my team members?

4. What five steps could I take to help my team members consistently strive to improve reciprocal commitment to and caring about their own people?

5. Without assigning the challenge to human resources, what five steps could the company as a whole take to improve its commitment to its employees, and consistently demonstrate that the company cares about its people?

CHAPTER NINE

THE MANY FACES OF COMPENSATION

While earning potential is always going to be an important aspect of a job, the company's culture is what motivates and inspires workers on a daily basis.

—Nina McQueen, LinkedIn vice president
of benefits and experience

Historically, compensation was *the* primary driver in the workplace, but according to Jordan Yadoo, writing on economics for the Bloomberg website, times have sure changed. In October 2018, Yadoo reported that Harvard, Rand Corp., and UCLA co-researchers found that "Americans are willing to give up 'substantial' earnings in exchange for non-wage perks and benefits."[50]

That's not to say that compensation isn't an important incentive for everyone; it is. We all deserve to be paid an appropriate wage for

---

50   Jordan Yadoo, "Americans Are Willing to Forgo a 56% Pay Raise for Best Job Perks," Bloomberg, October 31, 2018, https://www.bloomberg.com/news/articles/2018-10-31/americans-willing-to-forgo-a-56-pay-raise-for-best-job-perks?utm_campaign=news&utm_medium=bd&utm_source=applenews.

our work, and issues of underpayment continue to plague too many employees:

- In the US, women are still paid less than 70 cents for every dollar that men earn.

- In the US, minorities, youth, and older employees continue to struggle against pay discrimination or US minimum wage levels (the federal minimum wage does not rank anywhere near the top, globally).

- Employees continue to reveal that they are taken for granted financially or exploited by their bosses (according to reporting websites such as Glassdoor and Indeed).

BE CLEAR, FAIR, AND OPEN

Companies recompensing well will always have an edge over companies that persist in taking unfair advantage of their workers. When it comes to compensation, my advice is: be clear, be fair, be open. Especially in today's full-employment environment, it's important to be fair in setting compensation levels that are at or above the market. And with the focus on transparency in business front and center, those organizations promoting clarity and openness in compensation have a decided edge with millennials, especially.[51]

When it comes to determining compensation policy, there are countless resources in the marketplace available to assist company leaders, HR professionals, and CFOs. In fact, there are bookstore

---

51 Chris Weller, "Millennials Are Breaking the One Big Salary Taboo—And It's Changing How Companies Operate," Business Insider, October 25, 2017, https://www.businessinsider.com/salary-not-taboo-for-millennials-changing-how-businesses-work-2017-10.

sections dedicated just to that purpose. A quick Google search for "employee compensation" results in endless articles, journals, and texts penned by experts on the subject.

For our purposes, though, Compensation is the final C that must be reviewed when you, the manager or company leader, run through your 7Cs checklist to uncover the root cause(s) of employee disengagement, discontent, and nonaccountability. If compensation issues are undermining your ability to inspire accountability in your team members and workers, those issues must be faced and met squarely. No amount of effort on your part will convince a financially unappreciated and thus disengaged employee that you value his or her contributions to your company. And no matter how big the carrot seems, most employees today (including salespeople) won't walk in the door without a base salary on which they can comfortably subsist. Even a purpose-driven millennial will defect to a company with clearer, fairer, and more open compensation principles and practices. It's only a matter of time.

WHAT IS COMPENSATION IN THE AGE OF MILLENNIALS?

Though they are known to be purpose driven in their job quests, millennials (and doubtless the generations coming up behind them) are savvy enough to school for and gravitate to the business sectors that pay them the highest in-the-door salaries—and offer them the best benefits and perks. Tech-related, health care, and pharmaceutical companies are high-paying magnets for these workers, while retail, consumer products companies, government, education, and nonprofits lose these workers to the better-paying sectors, according to media reports.[52]

Remember our West Coast staffing company CEO, Isabel (introduced in Chapter Four), who found herself with 80 percent millennials on staff who are not driven by hefty sales commissions? "They're just not as money motivated as the previous generations," she protested to me. "Yes, our former hires had low base salaries, but the super-high commissions motivated those people to work like crazy. They earned a lot of money, which was good for us and good for them. Now everyone wants to go home at 5:00 p.m. and have a beer with friends. If money doesn't drive these new hires, what are we supposed to do?"

Even venerable sectors like law and investment banking can't lure enough millennials, though the promise of highly lucrative careers in those professions was so enticing to boomers. But millennials are impatient; they can't stomach the years of "slaving" required to grab those gold rings, especially when their years of tech immersion—playing video games, coding, and social media expertise, for instance—have made them so attractive to the other business segments willing to court them.

What's more, if a millennial is going to sign on for an eighty-hour workweek, he'll likely be biking to a Silicon Valley campus that can feed him, offer him diversion and exercise, supply his dry cleaning, and look after his pet. (Or, he'll be starting his own company: millennials are exceedingly entrepreneurial.) He might even sign on with a company like L.L. Bean, which recently teamed up with shared workspace innovator Industrious Boston to try out

---

52 Karsten Strauss, "When Millennials Switch Jobs, Where Do They Go?" *Forbes, August 7, 2017,* https://www.forbes.com/sites/karstenstrauss/2017/08/07/when-millennials-switch-jobs-where-do-they-go/#5b6a6d0e354.

outdoor "offices" that enable their employees to perform their work in the great outdoors.[53]

The truth is, the higher-maintenance millennial will be opting for a job that offers lifestyle balance and is actually *fun. After all, workplace fun ranks high for millennials and for Best Places to Work companies such as Google, Twitter, and SAS, according to the Stanford University Press blog.*[54] A millennial probably won't yearn to be a suited-up McKinsey consultant hopping planes eighty hours a week to service clients while his potted plants shrivel back at his digs.

Conversely, the only reason a millennial will opt for a job with skimpy compensation is if it is a purpose-driven (socially conscious or environmentally focused) post, or a position with a purpose-driven company like Patagonia.[55] Many millennials do indeed want to save the planet and might be willing to live on a limited income (for a period of time) to do it. The question is: Is *your* company a purpose-driven organization? If not, building in socially driven purpose might be a valid consideration. Right now, though, your immediate challenge is to design compensation that can motivate and reward the desired behaviors of your employees and attract the best job candidates. The fact is, if you don't get the reward/incentive system right, it's hard to end up with the behavior you desire, or the candidates you need to grow your business.

So, what constitutes "compensation" these days? Is compensation solely about dollars? The answer is no. Compensation is only

53 Tessa Yannone, "L.L. Bean Launches Outdoor Co-Working Space on the Greenway," *Boston, August 7, 2017,* https://www.bostonmagazine.com/health/2018/07/10/ll-bean-outdoor-co-working/.

54 Bob Kulhan, "Millennials Just Want to Have Fun," Stanford University, January 24, 2017, http://stanfordpress.typepad.com/blog/2017/01/millennials-just-want-to-have-fun.html.

55 Recommended reading: Yvon Chouinard, *Let My People Go Surfing: The Education of a Reluctant Businessman* (New York: Penguin Books, 2005/2016).

one method by which you build in motivation and reward. In the twenty-first century, *compensation is anything that motivates and inspires.* You can compensate people in numerous ways beside salary and bonuses. You can compensate with generous health and retirement (401k) benefits and stock options, yet you can also compensate with additional offerings that represent great value to particular employees. Offerings such as:

- More free time (e.g., Friday afternoons off in the summer).
- Additional vacation time.
- Flexible work hours.
- Job sharing.
- The ability to work from home and/or not relocate.
- Training and assistance with career path development.
- Tuition support.
- On-campus perks such as workout facilities.
- Onsite daycare/nursing.
- Extended maternity leave.
- Paternity leave for fathers.
- Donation to employee charities and causes.
- Employee discounts.
- Vacation prizes for meeting goals (popular in sales).
- Awards and public recognition.

COMPENSATION CLARITY: THE TWO-WAY COMPENSATION CONVERSATION

Once again, the most effective way to understand what will best compensate your employees is to initiate a process of inquiry and two-way dialogue: ask your employees to reveal what forms of compensation have the greatest meaning to them.

Certainly, you could wait for the semiannual review to have the all-important, two-way compensation discussion. But two-way conversations are more likely and much more effective when they can occur spontaneously and be initiated by your employees themselves within a culture of safety that encourages such openness. In a safe culture, workers feel free to speak up and voice their compensation concerns or needs. In unsafe cultures, far too many managers and employers find themselves wondering why a valued employee suddenly departed for greener pastures. This is especially true in companies with millennial employees who tend to flee without first confronting their managers about issues such as compensation. A blindsided manager then wonders, "Why didn't she just tell me she felt under-compensated? I would have done something about it!"

Recently, I reached out to a cohort of employees selected from various client companies to find out how they would respond to the issue of compensation. The effort was an anecdotal exercise, not a formal study. It cut across a group of about two dozen employees mostly in their twenties and thirties, with a few respondents in their early forties. I posed an imaginary scenario in which my interviewees would not be able to achieve the salary/bonus package they most desired. The offering would come in under (though not alarmingly under) what they hoped for. I wanted to know what *other* forms of compensation would be almost as valuable, equally valuable, or more valuable to them than the dollars.

Their specific compensation suggestions were all across the board, but overwhelmingly the respondents pointed to *lifestyle balance* as equally or more important than actual salary/bonus dollars. Offerings leading the way: the ability to work from home, work flexible hours, and be offered training/assistance with career development. More free time (for instance, Friday afternoons off) was also appealing, because it would allow the respondents to pursue various avocations, interests, and causes that were important to them, and which could not easily be pursued on weekends.

Importantly, my little exercise highlighted generational characteristics that so many employers overlook: Millennials, for instance, trace few of the life-pattern footsteps of earlier generations. As we have discussed previously, they marry and build families much later than preceding generations. Because of that, they tend not to invest in cars and homes until a good deal later (if at all), and thus settle in cities where they can walk, bike, and take mass transit to enjoy the many interests (restaurants, bars, events) that their parents were too busy raising families to enjoy. In major metropolitan areas, their rents tend to be much higher (proportionately) than were their parents' mortgages. This is partially because a preponderance of housing units once occupied by couples with children now house young single professionals instead, placing housing at a premium in cities such as Boston, New York, San Francisco, Los Angeles, London, and Paris.

Millennials and younger generations also rely on services that previous generations did not: they order out, frequent gyms, and depend on car services like Uber and Lyft. Clearly, millennials lead expensive lives. Without families to raise, however, they find the wherewithal to do so. What millennials seek is convenience (workout facilities on the business campus, for instance) and time to pursue their many interests. With their preferences for compensation such as flextime, ability to work from home, and extra time off, my survey participants made the value of such compensatory elements clear. And because millennials highly regard mentoring and career/life assistance, my interviewees' penchant for training and assistance with career development was not surprising.

What do *your* employees value? What types of compensation are most meaningful to them? It's time to forge your own process of inquiry, enabling a two-way conversation wherein you truly listen. If you are a company leader, many of your employees' responses can inform important company-wide discussions about company culture. Yet even if a manager does not have the reach to shape enterprise-wide change, every manager needs to find new ways to attract the best job candidates, and better engage and retain existing employees. That's why *all* managers need to think seriously about compensation change that can be initiated locally:

- Can you offer some of your team members the option to work at home as needed or on various weekdays?

- Can you create greater opportunities for mentoring, training, and career-path guidance in your own group?

- Can you use Fridays off or an extra vacation week as incentives for meeting group goals, even if time off is not a company-wide policy blessed by HR?

You probably can, and in the process, you will not only be more effectively compensating your own people, you will be creating an internal model for essential cultural change within your organization.

ALIGNING COMPENSATION WITH DESIRED BEHAVIOR

It's clear that compensation is a powerful motivator of behavior. It can motivate employees to work extremely hard and become high producers. Unfortunately, money can motivate bad as well as good behavior. Bringing on a talented hire at a competitive salary and then meting out only cost of living increases (or less) in ensuing years doesn't recognize hard work; it sends the opposite message, disappointing and demotivating a valuable employee. The resulting behavior will generally be disappointing as well—if the worker even stays on board. Poorly conceived, compensation can even motivate the worst kind of behavior: it can induce people to lie, cheat, and steal.

In short, attention *must* be paid to the precise behavior that may be motivated by the compensation plan put in place. Which behaviors do you want to see? For example, do you want to see *individual* behaviors and goals, *team* behaviors and goals, or both? Are bottom-line results your only concern, or will you be assessing additional goals? One good question to ask yourself as you consider the behaviors that might result from your compensation

THE MISALIGNMENT OF COMPENSATION WITH DESIRED BEHAVIORS COMPLETELY UNDERMINES THE OVERARCHING GOAL OF THE COMPANY TO SUCCEED AND GROW.

package: What specific goals do you imagine Wells Fargo had established when the company set its sales teams on the public like hounds on foxes? What results criteria or audits might have helped control the resulting employee behavior, other than an ongoing tally of sales volume or credit accounts opened?

Think about this: in some company cultures, where underpaying employees is commonplace, workers can feel so undervalued that they disengage early on and make the *customer* the recipient of their compensation dissatisfaction. Paradoxically, the misalignment of compensation with desired behaviors completely undermines the overarching goal of the company to succeed and grow.

In some companies where employees are undeniably undersalaried (say, in start-ups or in verticals such as education or journalism, with historically low salaries), compensating advantages such as autonomy may be nuanced, but are nonetheless powerful. In a very real sense, the plus of being effectively trained to "run your own business" is worth a great deal to many software gurus, teachers, and writers, for instance. Is autonomy a legitimate aspect of compensation? It is when it is one of the attractive benefits that is rolled into "Here's what you get for working here." Autonomy, for instance, is one of the reasons that certain individuals are attracted to sales: it represents the two-fold allure of (a) commissions limited by no one but yourself and (b) the prospect of being virtually your own boss.

Most of us have experienced frustrating interactions speaking on the phone with classically underpaid customer service reps who were unhelpful largely because they had limited authority to resolve complex or difficult issues and could only work off of their scripts. Not only are these unfortunate people paid a meager base wage, they are set up to fail to resolve issues, ensuring that they work with angry customers they cannot make happy (while also watching their commissions evaporate).

How different a phone interaction is with a Ritz-Carlton Hotels rep, empowered to spend up to $1,000 to resolve a customer's issue with no authorization needed. Along with a compensation package that includes generous base pay, comprehensive health benefits, employee discounts at Marriott properties, and 401k matching, Ritz-Carlton customer service reps receive a significant level of autonomy as a condition of their employment. This means that, empowered to succeed and actually *earn* her commissions, an Ritz-Carlton customer service rep can make $55,000 annually (according to employee feedback on Glassdoor[56]) while yearly income for US customer service reps in general falls within the $30,000 range (according to Salary[57]).

Most significantly, customer service reps whose compensation is aligned with desired behavior deal with customers who end up thrilled with the caring "face of the company" they encounter. The reps are not solely in the business of customer service; their well-honed skills qualify them as customer retention pros and experts in building customer loyalty. Yes, these valuable reps' salaries may not be as high as those of on-site executives who commute to headquarters daily. But their compensation for not pursuing a more conventional career may include:

- The ability to find work after others are "aged out."

- Flexible hours and days.

- The ability to work from home.

- Time off to visit or care for family members as needed.

- Money saved on gas, lunches, and business wardrobes.

---

56 "Ritz-Carlton Customer Service Hourly Pay," Glassdoor, accessed January 7, 2019, https://www.glassdoor.com/Hourly-Pay/Ritz-Carlton-Customer-Service-Hourly-Pay-E3433_D_KO13,29.htm.

57 "Salary for Customer Service Representative in the United States," Salary, accessed January 7, 2019, https://www1.salary.com/Customer-Service-Representative-I-Salary.html.

- Autonomy (including the ability to use one's own skills and discretion to problem-solve and, in the process, create customer loyalty).

For many people, these kinds of factors—nuanced or not—constitute an irresistible compensation package. By aligning compensation planning with desired behavior, enterprises such as the Ritz-Carlton Hotel Company do not waver from their mission, vision, and values; they never use compensation to—unwittingly or not—encourage behavior that might undermine their overarching objectives. (Ritz-Carlton is third on the 2018 HelpScout list of eight US companies with best customer service.[58] That list also includes Trader Joe's, JetBlue, Rackspace, and CVS. Among *Forbes*'s top ten[59] are Publix, Chick-fil-A, Lexus, Costco, and Amazon.)

TIP: Compensate Teams *and* Individuals

Do you want a truly collaborative team? Then make sure your compensation reinforces team behavior, not just the behavior of individuals. Today, many companies add team bonuses to compensation, not just to motivate collaboration, but to prevent large-scale disengagement. Noted one very smart senior-level manager: "I realized that in rewarding only the salespeople—which is classic—we had a very real problem. Other team members were

---

58 Gregory Ciotti, "8 Companies with Exceptional Customer Service," HelpScout, accessed January 7, 2019, https://www.helpscout.net/helpu/exceptional-customer-service-companies/.

59 Christopher Elliot, "These Companies Have the Best Customer Service," *Forbes, July 11, 2018,* https://www.forbes.com/sites/christopherelliott/2018/07/11/these-companies-have-the-best-customer-service-heres-why/#5c7902e9b80a.

getting the message that the sales people were the stars, because their job was to bring in the accounts. Whatever the others contributed seemed not to 'count' as much. Yet, without their contributions, the team as a whole would be sunk. Setting up a reward system that tells everyone that we're in this as a team *as well as* individuals has proved to be one of our most effective ways to align compensation with the working behaviors that lead to success."

OPENNESS ABOUT COMPENSATION

Traditionally, companies have frowned on the sharing of compensation information with or among employees. In many organizations, the act of sharing compensation information is an infraction that can warrant dismissal. Still, an employee's need to know how his compensation ranks with the external or internal market is tantamount to having a compass to guide him in the wild: Is he within range of others? Selling himself cheaply? Or is he asking too much and pricing himself out of a job?

The need for access to compensation information is so widespread that it became a driver behind many job and career websites that sprang up in recent years. Site visitors can get a quick read on salary ranges for comparable jobs in various parts of the country or the globe and also access salary range information from current and ex-employees of companies they are considering—or of companies that compete with their own.

This information can be absolutely vital to a job applicant who is required to fill out an online application for an advertised post. The job aggregator Indeed, for example, screens applicants by salary range. Many applicants are taken aback by the "desired salary range" question. They are web-savvy enough to know that a response out of an employer's range will instantly filter out their application. The prospective employer will never even see their excellent qualifications for the posted job. Having a sense of the going rate for a particular position in advance will at least give them a shot at it.

Today, enlightened organizations have less fear about openness when it comes to compensation. They have to, if they want to attract and keep their millennial workers, for millennials have already smashed the taboo on money talk.[60] More and more, companies are directing their employees and potential hires to salary information available on the web. Truly progressive organizations even post current salaries[61] to help cut through salary ambiguity, but also to demonstrate to their people and the public at large that a culture of transparency, in and of itself, sets the company apart from competitors.

No matter how open a company is about its compensation and reward structure, openness about job expectations is also essential. In other words:

- What does the manager or organization *expect* for the compensation it offers?

- What is the up-to-date job description?

---

60   Chris Weller, "Millennials Are Breaking the One Big Salary Taboo—And It's Changing How Companies Operate," Business Insider, October 25, 2017, https://www.businessinsider.com/salary-not-taboo-for-millennials-changing-how-businesses-work-2017-10.

61   "18 Companies with Salaries You Can See *Before* Applying," Glassdoor, April 25, 2018, https://www.glassdoor.com/blog/companies-with-salaries/.

- How many hours per week will the employee be expected to work?

- How will the employee's performance be measured—is there a job scorecard?

- How often will that performance be reviewed?

Reality that doesn't jibe with expectation is a major cause of employee disengagement, and few compensation packages can make up for an employee's sense that she has been hoodwinked or has signed on for limitless obligations. Whether an employment contract and compensation agreement is written, verbal, or implied, smart managers are open and *specific* about job expectations when presenting compensation for the job at hand.

In the age of Glassdoor, the last thing you want is for your people to broadcast, "This is a sweatshop! They work people crazy hours and don't pay them!"

COMPENSATION VS. AN INTOLERABLE BOSS OR CULTURE

We can't close a 7Cs discussion about compensation without remembering that compensation of almost any kind can't make up for a boss who is impossible to work for. Compensation is not the number one reason people leave their jobs—an unappreciative and untenable boss or culture is. In my coaching practice, I have worked with the most senior level and highly remunerated managers, who have at times confided they could not work for their bosses (often the CEO of the company) for one more minute. These are valuable individuals who make millions for their organizations. Yet they dread each day of work, eventually believing that no level of pay and benefits can compensate them for their misery.

One coaching client, for instance, confided to me: "A staffer I want to promote is better than the people at levels above him; he's doing outstanding work. I'm giving him an 'exceeds expectation' in his review, and I want to bump him up to the next pay level. HR says I've already used my 10 percent this year, so I went back to my boss and I told him we have a flight risk with this staffer. I said, 'I'm going to lose my best hire unless I can bump him up.' But my boss said, 'I've already been to HR twice and the answer is no.' How can I keep people I can't recompense for their work? How can I work for a company that ties my hands and doesn't appreciate me or my people?"

FINAL WORDS

Be clear about what people can expect from you and what you expect from them. Be fair in setting compensation levels that are at or near or above the market. Know what the market is and be willing to talk about it. And be open to dialogue with your people so that they can question how you arrived at the right salary for this job and why you think the compensation package is fair—and maybe why *they* don't.

TAKE ACTION: REASSESS HOW YOU COMPENSATE YOUR PEOPLE

To help you see compensation as more than just salary and benefits, start with these four steps:

1. **Check out the competition.** Make a list of your leading competitors for the best hires.

Then, visit websites like Glassdoor and Indeed. Find out what your competition offers its job candidates and current employees to get them on board and keep them happy, valued, and engaged. How could you meet or exceed such compensation?

2. **Motivate behavior.** What behavior(s) should your compensation motivate? If you have put together a possible compensation package per number one above, does each aspect motivate the best possible behavior? Look carefully: Might any of the items on your list actually encourage negative behavior that could sink your group or company ship?

3. **Offer powerful, but nuanced, benefits.** Don't underestimate subtler, yet powerful, benefits you can offer that your competition may not. Autonomy and empowerment, for instance, may directly result in dollars, especially for customer service reps and the like. Think carefully: What do you and your company extend to employees that adds greater potential for career success and satisfaction?

4. **Be open about compensation context.** Are you able to help place your offering in legitimate external/internal market context for potential hires or current employees? Arming your people with accurate market or company

information to help them best assess their compensation benefits both employer and employee. Think about your own satisfaction purchasing a car today as opposed to many years back: Does today's auto price transparency make you more likely to feel good about your purchase, or more likely to suspect that you've been duped? Openness is trending across business everywhere, because it serves both sides entering into a contract—including employers and employees.

YOUR ACCOUNTABILITY EDGE IN THE AGE OF MILLENNIALS–AND BEYOND

If you don't know where you are going, you'll end up someplace else.

—Yogi Berra, great American catcher, manager, and coach for the New York Yankees

Everyone who has ever run a company or managed people who work for a company has faced hair-pulling moments of wondering why some employees cannot do the jobs they were hired to do, do them well, and do them with some level of gladness or engagement. For lack of a better word, the business world calls the state of promised job delivery *accountability*. We said we would do the work, we committed to doing the work, and as promised, here are the results you expected.

Accountability sounds pretty cut-and-dried, yet in reality is anything but.

For many years, I have worked shoulder-to-shoulder with company leaders and senior-level management people to improve results in the workplace and shape more effective leadership. In particular, I have focused on the expectations and disappointments around accountability and, in the process, have helped many top executives resolve their own personal job woes.

In all that time, I can say this: human beings in the workplace have never ceased to fascinate me.

I suspect that I am continually captivated because I have spent a large part of my life guiding others to not just go through the motions of their work lives, but to be *inspirational.* What could be more human than to inspire others to love what they do?

As it happens, inspiring accountability (rather than demanding it) can be life changing for all involved, in three very important ways:

- One, it can catapult an enterprise toward levels of success that were previously unimaginable.

- Two, the skill of inspiring accountability can be a career maker for the manager who acquires it.

- Three, the recipient of such inspiration is blessed, for he will love what he does every day he is at work.

THE 7CS EDGE IN A MILLENNIAL WORLD

It would indeed be magical if any business-guidance book constituted a complete and total solution to the workplace challenges of our age. But just as with the concepts of demanding accountability versus inspiring it, it is the *human* touch that makes forging change in the workplace most powerful and enduring. That's why although surveying one's team members is an indisputably helpful step, a more profound action would be to speak with each of them, one-on-one. To note their body language and hear the tone of their words. To respond with immediacy. To strike a chord of understanding and in return be energized by your own new awareness. It turns out that, in the workplace as everywhere else in life, the value of relating as human beings is incalculable.

That's why there is no underestimating what intimate experience with workplace and behavioral change brings to the table. A coach who has come up against accountability issues again and again and has spent years honing the best possible solutions is not unlike the surgeon who has performed a procedure hundreds of times and perfected it in the process.

That said, short of working closely with you and your teams in your own workplace, through this book I hand you a tested, proprietary structure that represents the most successful healing techniques I have innovated while working inside top US enterprises. With the 7Cs, you'll no longer find yourself "someplace else" as Yogi Berra warned in the quotation at the beginning of this chapter. Instead, you'll be on the path to precisely where you need to be, armed with a decisive accountability edge in your marketplace.

> A COACH WHO HAS COME UP AGAINST ACCOUNTABILITY ISSUES AGAIN AND AGAIN AND HAS SPENT YEARS HONING THE BEST POSSIBLE SOLUTIONS IS NOT UNLIKE THE SURGEON WHO HAS PERFORMED A PROCEDURE HUNDREDS OF TIMES AND PERFECTED IT IN THE PROCESS.

How powerful is that edge? One client crystallized our work together when she remarked that it "completely flipped the accountability paradigm of managers blaming employees and getting nowhere." Another recently confessed that the structure is so relevant right now that it's practically "the secret sauce to managing and motivating millennials!" Still another has termed my method "learning to speak 'millennial'—like John Gray's Mars and Venus, but for today's managers."

Whether your challenges are focused on millennials or not, my methods are designed to help companies, groups, teams, and their leaders move in wholly new directions, breaking through the shackles of disengagement and nonaccountability. What my countless client engagements all have in common is my use of what has become a clear, targeted, and proven checklist: a framework of seven key issues for examination that will enable any company leader or manager to quickly zero in on precisely where the root causes of nonaccountability lie.

Are your people disengaged and unproductive because your **company culture** is damaged or seriously flawed? Did it evolve without a plan, and is it not relevant or hospitable to your incoming workers, now largely millennials? If so, what can you do about that? How can you begin to assess the chinks in that culture and their impact on what your company, group, or team (or all three) need to achieve?

> DO YOU KNOW HOW TO DEMONSTRATE THAT MOST MAGICAL OF LEADERSHIP ATTRIBUTES: THAT YOU SINCERELY CARE ABOUT THOSE WHO WORK FOR YOU, AND WHO WANT TO WORK HARD FOR YOU?

Are your employees unable to deliver on their commitments because **clarity** from management (you!) is lacking, preventing workers from performing as you expect them to? Are you burying your well-meaning employees with **capacity** overload? Do you not care to know if their workloads are realistic? Or, are there **competency** issues at bay: workers who need more training, should be recast in other roles, or were unsuitable (but cheap) at point of hire?

Are you inadvertently eroding the **confidence** of the people who initially had intended only to succeed in their work for you? Have you (unintentionally or intentionally) ignored their requests for the mentoring, support, and increased levels of responsibility that would have helped them grow in their roles? Have you noticed that millennials in particular respond to greater support in this area?

Can you honestly say that your behavior as a company leader demonstrates your full **commitment** to your employees and their success? Conversely, do you have the skill to elicit their highest levels of commitment to you, their teams, and the company as a whole? Do you know how to demonstrate that most magical of leadership attributes: that you sincerely care about those who work for you, and who want to work hard for you?

Finally, do you have a real sense of what genuinely constitutes clear, fair, and open **compensation** in this age of millennials? Do you know how to reward and motivate today's workers? Do you know what kind of "payment for services rendered" attracts and engages generations that are unlike their predecessors?

The 7Cs detailed in this book describe what portions of an in-person coaching engagement with you and your company might look like. And, as often happens, the 7Cs interconnect in ways you may never have expected. Yet with a greater understanding of each of the Cs, you can launch your own root-cause investigation, open your own process of two-way dialogue and inquiry (the direct route to accountability), and lay much of the groundwork for remarkable improvement.

OPTIMIZING YOUR CURRENT AND FUTURE WORKPLACE

The pundits tell us that our workplace populations will be 75 percent millennial by 2025, but many of my clients report that their workplaces are already just about there. Certainly, some businesses attract millennials more than others: Right now, millennials are flocking to tech and health care, for instance. And though tech companies tend to be more tuned in to their millennials (many are start-ups headed by millennial or Gen X innovators), other sectors such as health care are more conventional business models now struggling to "speak millennial." Still other verticals—investment banking and finance, for instance—can't even get millennials to sign on or stay on board if they do. Companies in those sectors have an urgent need for the 7Cs, to help them cut through company cultures and management paradigms that *must* be flipped quickly—or else.

Whatever your workplace picture or population, there is just no doubt that disengagement—and the death of accountability it spawns—is your enemy. Employees not committed to performing for their bosses make their companies noncompetitive and can actually speed an enterprise's departure from its marketplace. Your current *modus operandi* may be to demand and command accountability, but that approach is counterproductive and is wasting precious time in the scheme of your company's—and your own—success. It doesn't have to be that way. Bring your 7Cs framework for change to the table, work it zealously, and be amazed. Even in this most challenging age of millennials, you *can* Inspire Accountability!

FINAL THOUGHTS ON LEADERSHIP

Effective leadership has never been more important than it is today in this age of rapid technological and social change. Leaders need to make difficult strategic decisions and determine how they will finance and execute their plans. This requires great analytical and problem-solving skills and the ability to recruit great people and clearly communicate their roles and responsibilities. However, these skills alone don't make a great leader. Leadership is all about getting things done through people. In today's age of educated, well-informed millennial workers and historically low unemployment, the balance of power has shifted from the employer to the employee. The job of leadership has changed from telling people what to do and holding them accountable to inspiring people to do the things you want them to do on their own and out of their own desire. This requires aligning employees with your mission, vision, and values; casting people in roles that play to their strengths; and making work meaningful and rewarding. It also means eliciting commitment by demonstrating your care and concern for the well-being, development, and happiness of your employees.

Leaders today need to change the skills they value most from:

- Talking and telling to asking and listening.

- Demanding and controlling to influencing and persuading.

- Demanding "no excuses" to insisting on "no surprises."

- Commanding to collaborating.

- Focusing on tasks to focusing on people and how they feel about themselves when they work for you.

- Being too busy to care about people's personal lives to being caring, concerned, and empathetic.

- Focusing on what's in it for the company to what's in it for employees and society.

- Managing to coaching.

The 7Cs provide a roadmap for inquiry that can lead to effective leadership in these challenging times. Remember, leadership is all about getting things done through people.

OUR SERVICES

Ken Estridge & Associates provides business and executive coaching. Business coaching services are focused on helping privately held companies with revenues of $10 million to $500 million employ best practices for scaling up their companies in the areas of strategy, people, execution, and cash. Ken helps clients develop effective growth strategies that accelerate sales and increase profitability. He helps them create high-performance teams, improve leadership effectiveness, and improve the company's efficiency and consistency of execution. Ken facilitates monthly, quarterly, and annual team meetings to ensure the implementation of these best practices. Ken also provides executive coaching to the CEOs of business coaching clients.

Executive coaching services are focused on improving the leadership skills of mid-level and senior executives in large companies (most of which are Fortune 500 Companies, some are large privately held companies). Executive coaching is focused on developing the soft skills of getting things done through people. This includes improving influence skills, increasing executive presence, improving communication, developing high-performance teams, and ensuring accountability for results. Ken's work also includes onboarding newly hired executives and maximizing an executive's career progression within large firms. Ken also speaks about effective leadership and inspiring accountability at industry conferences and events.

For more information on Ken's services, visit **www.kenestridge.com**

Printed in the USA
CPSIA information can be obtained
at www.ICGtesting.com
JSHW012027140824
68134JS00033B/2910